Sounds
may be 0...
To something.
Happy Birthday
YELG '07

HOW TO LIVE WELL WITHOUT OWNING A CAR

HOW TO
LIVE WELL
WITHOUT
OWNING
A CAR

save money, breathe easier, and get more mileage out of life

chris balish

TEN SPEED PRESS
Berkeley | Toronto

Ten Speed Press
PO Box 7123
Berkeley, California 94707
www.tenspeed.com

Distributed in Canada by Ten Speed Press Canada.

Design by Kate Basart/Union Pageworks
Illustrations copyright © by Andy Singer unless otherwise noted
Illustration on page viii copyright © by Dennis Draughon
Illustrations on pages 38, 76, 177, 200, and 208 copyright © by Sue Clancy

Library of Congress Cataloging-in-Publication Data
Balish, Chris.
  How to live well without owning a car : save money, breathe easier, and get more mileage out of life / Chris Balish.
    p. cm.
  Includes index.
  ISBN-13: 978-1-58008-757-5
  ISBN-10: 1-58008-757-4
1.Automobile ownership—United States. 2. Automobiles—Economic aspects.
  3. Finance, Personal—United States. I. Title.
HE5623.B35 2006
332.024—dc22
                          2006011679

Printed in the United States of America on recycled paper (40% PCW)

2 3 4 5 6 7 8 9 10 — 10 09 08 07 06

Contents

ACKNOWLEDGMENTS

More than two hundred people contributed to this book. I want to thank literary super-agent Laurie Abkemeier, whose tenacity and enthusiasm for this project never waned. I am grateful to Brie Mazurek and all of the forward-thinking folks at Ten Speed Press for daring to challenge America's car culture with me. I want to thank my researcher and fact-checker extraordinaire, my father, Tom Balish. Thank you to Candice and Kevin Kelsey and to Tommy and Peep Balish for their belief in this project and for their insightful criticism. Thanks to Jeanie Wren, one of the best proofreaders ever, for her early review of the manuscript. Thanks to copy editor Kristi Hein, who challenged assumptions, oppugned arguments, and asked the tough questions, making this a better book. Thanks to Tommy Lupo for his big-picture critique. Special thanks to the talented artists who contributed their work to this book: Andy Singer, Sue Clancy, and Dennis Draughon. Many thanks, also, to the hundreds of individuals I interviewed for this book, especially for agreeing to let me quote their personal stories and private financial information. Thanks to Becky, who tolerated my obsession with this project for more than a year. Thanks to Eric, Nick, and Martine at Club 406—what can I say? And finally, I owe a special debt of gratitude to Georgia Rae, Gus, and Anton, who have inspired me to leave the world a better place—ideally with many fewer cars.

INTRODUCTION

Despite what $20 billion of automobile advertising every year would have us all believe, buying or leasing a car, truck, or SUV is the worst financial move most people make in their lifetime. And they make this mistake again and again, at a cost of literally hundreds of thousands of dollars. As you will see in the coming chapters, cars devour cash, increase debt, reduce savings, and make financial freedom difficult to achieve.

This book suggests taking a different path—a car-free path. The program in these pages will show you how to live a full, active life without owning a car. And without a car to pay for, practically anyone can get out of debt, save money, and achieve financial freedom. The truth is that tens of millions of working Americans do *not* need to own a car. One basic premise of this book is that if you can get to work reliably without a car, you don't need to own one.

Are there exceptions? Sure, plenty. Families with children may find it difficult, though not impossible, to live car-free (see chapter 28). Outside sales representatives who use their cars to make sales calls would have a hard time not owning one. Construction workers who haul heavy tools need their pickup trucks. People who live in rural areas not served by public transit might find car-free living difficult. And anyone with special medical needs or demanding family responsibilities probably needs to own a car.

There's no doubt that cars, trucks, and SUVs are useful tools. They provide instant, on-demand transportation at a moment's notice. They can haul heavy loads and help you run errands. And they can whisk you out of town for a weekend away. That's why this book does *not* suggest that you never use a car or never ride in one.

This book simply argues that millions of Americans can get along just fine and save a fortune by not *owning* a car. The few times a year when you do need one you can rent or use car sharing.

Living car-free in America is not difficult, but it does require some mild lifestyle changes. This book will walk you through the process step-by-step. The strategies in this book will put you on the car-free path to financial freedom; or, if you do not wish to get rid of your car entirely, this book will help you save money by using your car less. So even if living "car-free" isn't your style, this book can show you how to live happily "car-lite."

PART ONE

Why You're Better Off Not Owning a Car

CHAPTER I

The Car-Free Way to Financial Freedom

> *"Your car is no longer a chariot of freedom; it's a money-sucking horse that gets you to the office."*
>
> —*Men's Health* MAGAZINE

If you currently own or lease a car, truck, or SUV, this book has the power to give you the equivalent of a $5,000 to $10,000 raise. Following the program in these pages can help you slash your monthly expenses, pay off your credit cards, build an investment portfolio, save for a house, and possibly pay off your mortgage early. You could even become a millionaire, or retire at age forty. Regardless of your income level, this book can help you keep more of your money and lead a richer life.

And financial benefits are just the beginning. You'll also learn how not owning a car is liberating, rewarding, and fun. Without a car to constantly take care of, you'll have fewer hassles, lower stress, less aggravation, and less to worry about. You may even find you have more free time. With no car in your life you may also improve your health, get more exercise, lose weight, and sleep better. In other words, you'll be happier, healthier, and *much* wealthier.

Best of all, practically anyone can live happily without owning a car—or as many people call it, living "car-free." This program is not abstract theory. It's not a fringe concept applicable to a select few. It is a broad-based, step-by-step process that almost anyone in mainstream America can follow to start saving money right away. Even if you're convinced you "need" a car, this program may change your mind.

What This Book Is

How to Live Well without Owning a Car is a personal finance and lifestyle book. It is a simple program that can dramatically improve your finances, your quality of life, and your peace of mind. According to *Kiplinger's Personal Finance* magazine, the best way to cut costs and save money is to go after one big expense, rather than a bunch of little ones. This book will show you how. And it's a lot easier than you think.

This book isn't written for people who live in New York City, where it's common not to own a car. The program is designed for people who live in the rest of America: in cities like Omaha, Phoenix, Los Angeles, San Francisco, Boston, St. Louis, Cincinnati, Chicago, Philadelphia, Salt Lake, Seattle, Miami, Sacramento, Washington, D.C., and so on. You can also live well without a car in smaller towns like Oxford, Ohio; Columbia, Missouri; and Eugene, Oregon.

The purpose of this book is to show you one heck of an easy way to save a ton of money.

CAR-FREE IN PORTLAND, OREGON

Because I don't own a car and haven't had to make car and insurance payments, or pay for gas, I have been able to save literally about $65,000. Instead of spending it on a car, this money has gone into my house and rental property (duplex) that I own, as well as helped me start a retirement account. Plus, once I started commuting by bicycle I lost twenty-five pounds!

—Linda Ginenthal, 45

Furthermore, this book is about living well without *owning* a car. It doesn't mean you won't ride in one or drive one occasionally. You will. You may even decide to keep your car, but use it less. This book will show you how.

Who Should Read This Book

Anyone who owns or leases a car or truck should read this book. If you have two or more cars, read it tonight! You should also read this book if:

- You're fed up with high gas prices
- You think owning a car is a hassle
- You have financial problems
- You worry about money
- You have credit card debt, student loans, or personal loans
- You long for the freedom and serenity of a debt-free lifestyle

With no exaggeration, this book can change your financial life, even if you go car-free for only a short time. But it's not just for people with troubled finances. This book is for you if:

- You're a renter and you want to save for a down payment on a house
- You want to pay off your mortgage in ten years, instead of thirty
- Your goal is to retire from full-time work in your forties
- You just want to work less and have more free time

Or maybe you feel your life is too complicated. Going car-free can simplify your life in one bold step. You'll have fewer bills to pay, less paperwork to do, and fewer complications in your life.

CAR-FREE IN GLENDALE, MISSOURI

Living car-free would be possible for most people if they put their minds to it and are willing to change their routines. I would say I'm saving about $500 a month on the usual suspects: gas, maintenance, repairs, car insurance, payments, personal property tax, license plates, inspection, city sticker. Ahhh, how glad I am to bid it all farewell!

—Rudy Schwarz, 53, architect

If you've already adopted a car-free or car-lite lifestyle, this book will help you maximize enjoyment, minimize hassle, and boost personal fulfillment. And if you follow the steps in chapter 22, your social life will soar.

Americans Spend One-Fifth of Their Income on Cars

According to the U.S. Bureau of Labor Statistics 2003 Consumer Expenditure Survey, the average American spends eighteen cents of every dollar earned on transportation. And 98 percent of that transportation spending is for "the purchase, operation, and maintenance of automobiles." That makes our cars the second largest expense behind housing. And by the way, that 18 percent figure may be low; it was calculated using the average price of gasoline in the year 2003, which was $1.55 per gallon.

Other research has also shown that Americans spend a big chunk of their income on cars. According to a 2004 American Automobile Association study, the average American spends $8,410 per year to own a vehicle. That's equal to $700 per month! The figure includes car payments, insurance, gas, oil, car washes, registration fees and taxes, parking, tolls, and repairs. You'll see those average AAA numbers used to calculate some of the financial examples later in this book. But, of course, "average" does not necessarily mean typical, and the amount Americans spend on their cars varies widely. The only way to know for sure how going car-free will affect *your* bottom line is to run the numbers for yourself. A worksheet in the next chapter will walk you through the calculations. But for now, just think about how your life would change if you had hundreds more dollars to spend (or save) every month.

CAR-FREE IN SANTA CRUZ, CALIFORNIA

I have been car-free since 1992. I have saved $150,000 since I sold my car, while earning between $5 and $15 per hour and working only twenty to forty hours a week. I heartily recommend car-free living. The adjustment can be hard to make, but the process itself is meaningful and leads to a better life.

—Micah Posner, 37, director of a nonprofit

CAR-FREE IN MINNEAPOLIS, MINNESOTA

I was seriously thinking about buying a car, but when I crunched the numbers I realized I would be better off doing without the car and buying a house instead. The fact that I don't own a car allowed me to qualify for a mortgage to buy a home on a small nonprofit salary. The rest is history. The house is a much better investment than the car would have been. Now I'm on track to retire at age fifty. Forget about the Volkswagen Bug and its dashboard flower. It's a lie.

—Matthew Lang, 29, community organizer

Show Me the Money

Let's consider what would happen if you invested your money, instead of spending it on a car. Are you ready for some shocking numbers? That AAA average annual cost to own a car of $8,410 invested at an 8 percent annual return over thirty years would be worth $1,043,251.

So if you adopt a car-free lifestyle over the long term, quite possibly you could become a millionaire. Imagine, a million-dollar net worth *just by not owning a car*! And that doesn't include any other savings or 401(k) money you might be investing.

On the other hand, thirty years is a long time. So what if you live car-free for a shorter period? Based on AAA's numbers ($700 a month) and an 8 percent annual return, going car-free would still have a dramatic impact on your finances.

TIME	CAR-FREE SAVINGS	WHAT YOU COULD DO WITH THAT MONEY
\$700 A MONTH INVESTED AT AN 8 PERCENT ANNUAL RETURN		
3 months	$2,100	Establish an emergency rainy-day fund
6 months	4,200	Fund an IRA retirement account
I year	8,410	Pay off credit card debt
2 years	18,153	Make a down payment on a house
3 years	28,374	Start a business or buy rental property
5 years	51,433	Pay cash for a child's college education
10 years	128,062	Pay off your mortgage
20 years	412,314	Retire early or semi-retire from full-time work
30 years	1,043,251	Pop the cork—you're a millionaire!

As you can see, the longer you go without owning a car, the greater the financial benefit. So the key to successfully using this book to reach your financial goals is simple: you must not merely *survive* without a car, you must learn to *live well* without a car. If you apply the advice in this book in the way that works best for you, living car-free will be a joy, not a struggle, and you may never want to own a car again.

WHY 8 PERCENT?

I chose to use an 8 percent investment return in the examples above because the long-term average annual returns of investing in the stock market exceed 8 percent. For example, the average annual total return for the S&P 500 stock market index (as of January 31, 2006) is as follows: one year, 10.38 percent; three years, 16.42 percent; and ten years, 8.99 percent.

However, investing in the stock market involves considerable risk, and is best suited for long-term investment (five years or longer). Also, past performance is no guarantee of future returns. So investing in the stock market is certainly not suitable for everyone. Therefore, I have included additional examples in this book based on a 5 percent average annual return. Five percent is a more likely return for conservative

$700 A MONTH INVESTED AT A 5 PERCENT ANNUAL RETURN	
TIME	CAR-FREE SAVINGS
3 months	$2,100
6 months	4,200
1 year	8,595
2 years	17,631
3 years	27,131
5 years	47,616
10 years	108,756
20 years	288,058
30 years	583,668

CAR-FREE IN WASHINGTON, D.C.

This year I purchased a condo. Because I didn't have a car—or a car payment—more of my income could be used to qualify for a higher mortgage. So rather than spending $600 per month on a depreciating asset I was able to invest it in an appreciating one. At 5.75 percent interest my $600 per month supports over $100,000 in mortgage. In the eighteen months since I signed my purchase contract my place has appreciated 26 percent.

—Jeff Baker, 43, computer programmer

investors, or for short-term investors who are not investing in the stock market. It is always a good idea to seek professional financial advice before investing in the stock market or any other volatile investment vehicle.

The Car-Free Way to Financial Freedom

Have you ever dreamed of taking six months off work to travel the world? Or maybe taking a year off to write a book? Or quitting your job to go back to graduate school? Sadly, for most people these things are simply not possible because their monthly expenses are too high, and they don't have enough savings.

When you live car-free, your monthly expenses drop dramatically and your savings can skyrocket. This powerful combination can give you the freedom to live life on your terms. Hate your job? Then quit, and take your time finding a new one. Does your wife want to stay home and be a full-time mom? She can. Would you rather work for a nonprofit, even though it would require a pay cut?

THE TRUE COST OF OWNING AN SUV

The American Automobile Association's annual cost estimate of $8,410 is for an "average" car. And the total cost is based on the average price of gasoline in 2004, which was $1.83 per gallon. But SUVs are not average cars; they burn more fuel, cost more to buy, and they're more expensive to insure. According to AAA, here are the average annual costs to own some popular SUVs.

SUV MODEL	ANNUAL COST
2004 Chevy Tahoe	$10,406
2004 Jeep Grand Cherokee	9,985
2004 Ford Explorer	9,843
2004 Toyota Sequoia	9,787
2004 Acura MDX	9,690
2004 Dodge Durango	9,587

Do it. This is financial freedom: the ability to make life decisions not based on financial concerns. When you live car-free, you can have this type of financial freedom.

"He that can live sparingly need not be rich."

—BEN FRANKLIN

You *Can* Live Well without a Car

As you are beginning to see, there are enormous financial benefits to living car-free. You'll read about more of these benefits in chapter 2. But can you really live in America without owning a car? And can you maintain your normal activities and your normal social life? The answer to both questions is yes.

Despite the fact that we live in a car-centered culture, not only can you *live* without a car, you can *live well* without a car. And if you follow the hundreds of tips and strategies in this book, living car-free can become downright easy. You'll learn how to get to

---

CAR-FREE IN KAMLOOPS, BRITISH COLUMBIA

My wife and I sold our car in October 2002. While we had no trouble affording the expense, economically it didn't make any sense to carry such a high fixed cost. Now I ride my bike to work or take public transit. Once in a blue moon (every three or four months) we'll rent a car to handle long distances or heavy loads.

We're saving roughly $7,000 per year by not having a car. That money goes toward paying down our mortgage sooner. We bought a home two years ago and we'll have it paid off in three more years. Once the house is paid off, we'll have an additional $15,000 per year in disposable income. While we could afford to buy several cars, we can think of far more fun things to do with that kind of financial freedom.

Needless to say, we recommend a car-free lifestyle to everyone—especially people who are struggling with debt, people who are overweight, those who feel socially isolated, and anyone looking to do more for the environment.

Can anyone live without a car? Absolutely! Every circumstance has a car-free answer. Got kids? Get bikes with trailers. When the kids are old enough, buy bikes for them. Live too far from work? Move closer to work and ditch the car. Overweight or out of shape? Getting rid of your car will whip you into shape. People too easily buy into the myth that you must drive to survive. And it's just that, a myth.

—Lenard Segnitz, information technology manager

work, how to get your shopping and errands done, how to maintain a vibrant social life, and how to overcome car-free challenges with creativity. By following the step-by-step program in this book, you will soon be smiling on your way to the bank, instead of frowning on your way to the gas pump.

The way I see it, my job is to teach you everything you need to know to live in America without owning a car. Deciding what to do with all the money you're about to save is up to you.

CAR-FREE IN CAMBRIDGE, MASSACHUSETTS

I hear people talking about how they couldn't live without a car. Then a few conversations later, they'll complain that their job doesn't pay enough and they don't have any money, without seeing the connection. The money I've saved from living car-free has helped me fund things like bike trips to Ireland and visits to farms in Tuscany, Italy.

—Jeffrey Rosenblum, 37, consultant

CAR-FREE IN CHICAGO, ILLINOIS

I spent what seemed like a lot of money at the time (I paid $104,000 in 1990) to purchase a home inside Chicago, close enough to where I work that cycling is easy, I can walk if I must, and I can ride a train or a bus if weather is really foul. However, the big up-front expense turned into a huge bargain over the years. Many others are also now finding the same neighborhood desirable for the same reasons, and instead of an expense my home has become quite valuable. I don't have an exact value because I haven't sold it, but similar properties are currently selling for about $400,000.

—Todd Allen, 40, computer programmer

CAR-FREE IN PROVO, UTAH

Cars are depreciating assets. You buy a new or used car and keep plowing money into it, then at the end of the day you sell it for a fraction of what you paid for it. On the other hand, if you choose to spend more money on where you live, you are making an investment in an appreciating asset. When I invest that money into my home, that asset appreciates. My net worth has been growing at around $2,000 per month for the last two years as I pay down debt and accumulate savings. I couldn't be doing that if I were spending money on a car. I'm convinced that this is the biggest issue in this discussion that virtually nobody talks about.

—Travis Jensen, 29, engineer

CAR-FREE IN HARTFORD, CONNECTICUT

I finished my master's degree and paid for my doctorate with money that would have been used to own and support a car habit.

—Dr. Malaika Sharp, computer science instructor and martial arts instructor

CHAPTER 2

The True Financial Costs of Owning Your Car

"If you buy what you don't need,
you steal from yourself."

—SWEDISH PROVERB

Owning a car is an enormous financial drain—one that millions of Americans could easily avoid. When you buy a new car you are spending thousands of dollars on an asset that will lose 20 percent of its value the day you buy it, lose another 10 to 15 percent of its value each year thereafter, require you to go into debt to pay for it, make you pay interest on the amount you borrowed to buy it, and force you to spend hundreds of dollars a month to continue to own it.

Car ownership can quietly rob you of a secure retirement. It can destroy your ability to save for college, start a business, or invest for the future. It can prevent you from working less and enjoying life more. And most of all, it may deny you the peace of mind that comes with financial freedom.

Are You Clueless about Car Costs?

Cars are a serious drain on personal finances, but for some reason people don't see this. Most people have little idea just how much

---

CAR-FREE IN PITTSBURG, CALIFORNIA
I work full-time about five months a year. The rest of the year I am "retired."
I figure if I felt that I needed to own a car, I'd have to work full-time year-round.

—Bruce "Ole" Ohlson, 56, cement truck driver

their car is costing them. If you ask someone what they spend each month on housing, you'll get a pretty accurate answer. "My rent is $800, cable is $50, electricity is about $70, and phone is $65." But when you ask the same person how much their car costs each month, they generally have no clue. Or they just add up the car payment, gas, and insurance, believing that's all there is to it.

This gross underestimation of how expensive cars are to own is so widespread it's a national epidemic. This lack of understanding is fueled by an endless barrage of automobile advertising purposely designed to make cars seem more affordable

"Advertising: the science of arresting human intelligence long enough to get money from it."

—Stephen B. Leacock, economist

than they really are. Commercials that promise "A brand new car for $199 a month! Just $199 a month!" are so misleading they should be illegal.

CAR-FREE IN ST. LOUIS, MISSOURI

My decision to get rid of my truck was a financial one. While I could afford the payment, the insurance, the gas, and the occasional parking tickets, it relieved considerable pressure not to have to do so. So I sold my Ford Ranger pickup truck and found I could indeed live relatively easily without an automobile.

The many, many costs associated with cars add up so quickly and silently, usually you don't even notice them. You only notice how little money you have in your bank account and wonder why. Not having a car allowed me to move to a newer, nicer apartment in a better area—closer to work. And I can now easily afford to go out to dinner and movies.

My financial situation is also more predictable without an automobile. I never knew when something would break and cost anywhere from $50 to $1,000. In those situations I felt totally at the mercy of repair shops. Car-free life does require making small adjustments in your routine and how you accomplish certain tasks. But with a little creativity and knowledge I think almost anyone can live car-free. I highly recommend it.

—Marcel Fremont, 26, laboratory technician

How many college students do you know who are so broke they can only afford mac-n-cheese for dinner, yet they just bought a new car to get them to and from class? They probably thought, "I can afford $199 a month." How many working adults do you know who constantly complain about money problems, yet they just leased a brand-new SUV? The reality is that cars come with dozens of unavoidable expenses that the average car owner either doesn't notice, doesn't want to notice, or just accepts as part of life without giving any real thought to the consequences.

In this chapter we'll help you figure out what your car is really costing you. We'll begin with the obvious costs. Then we'll take a look at some not so obvious costs, like depreciation—a huge expense that most people don't understand. If you're a car owner, these expenses are quietly conspiring to steal your money and rob you of financial security.

Cars Cost Twice as Much as You Think

The first concept you have to grasp is that the amount of money it costs to *buy* a car is very different from the amount it costs to *own* a car. One of the best resources for computing the total cost to own a vehicle is the car-buying website www.edmunds.com. This highly regarded site primarily offers reviews and ratings of various car models.

"Gas. Maintenance. Warranty. What else is there?"

—Ad copy from a Jeep/ Chrysler television commercial, November 2005

But it also has one of the best car cost calculators I've seen. They call it True Cost to Own (TCO). You just select the year, make, and model, and Edmunds.com will tell you how much it will cost to own that vehicle over a five-year period. It's usually about double the purchase price.

Here's an example. A brand-new 2005 Ford Explorer XLS has a cash purchase price of $22,132. But according to Edmunds.com, the True Cost to Own that Explorer over five years is actually $44,177. So although your car payment may be around $400 per month, the actual amount being sucked out of your wallet is more than $700 per month.

Where is the difference coming from? To figure the true cost of owning a car, you must add up a lot more than just your monthly payment and insurance premiums. Edmunds.com includes the following costs in their calculations: depreciation, financing, insurance, taxes and fees, repairs, maintenance, and fuel for 15,000 miles per year. (Keep in mind the TCO does not include many other car-related expenses, such as parking, body repairs, AAA membership, and so on.)

CAR-FREE IN SAN FRANCISCO, CALIFORNIA

The reason many people think they need so much money is because they think they need a car. All the taxi rides, bike repairs, plane tickets, rental cars to get out of town, and bus passes add up to only a fraction of what car owners pay for their transportation. I pay about $600 per year for transportation, including everything but planes. Planes cost me about $1,000 per year for three to six trips. That totals $1,600—less than many car owners pay just for gas.

—Joel Pomerantz, 44, tour guide

2005 FORD EXPLORER XLS, PURCHASE PRICE: $22,132 TRUE COST TO OWN						
	YEAR 1	YEAR 2	YEAR 3	YEAR 4	YEAR 5	TOTAL
Depreciation	$10,924	$2,162	$1,902	$1,687	$1,513	$18,188
Financing	1,215	978	724	453	164	3,534
Insurance	1,014	1,049	1,086	1,124	1,163	5,436
Taxes & fees	1,679	51	51	51	51	1,883
Fuel	2,006	2,066	2,128	2,192	2,258	10,650
Maintenance	373	634	447	1,581	776	3,811
Repairs	0	0	98	235	342	675
Yearly totals	17,211	6,940	6,436	7,323	6,267	44,177

Source: Edmunds.com

In the example above, notice that the Explorer's value dropped by half in the first year alone, and by more than $18,000 over the five-year period. Depreciation expense is often overlooked completely when calculating a car's total cost, because a car owner never actually has to write a check payable to "depreciation." But make no mistake, you definitely pay for it. A portion of your car payment every month goes to cover some of this depreciation loss. So while you're making payments on a loan for a $22,000 SUV, at the end of five years you're left with a vehicle that's only worth $4,000. Spending $44,000 to end up with something worth $4,000 doesn't sound like a smart financial move to me.

So rather than spend $44,000 over five years on an SUV that drops in value every year, what would happen if you saved and invested that money over the same sixty months? If you earned an 8 percent annual return in five years you'd be sitting on more than $53,000 in cash. If you earned a 5 percent annual return you'd have more than $49,000 in the bank. Now that's a smart financial move.

What About Used Cars?

The main thing you're saving when you buy a used car is that big first-year hit in depreciation. All the other expenses remain. And some of what you save in depreciation expense you may lose in higher repair cost. Once again, according to Edmunds.com, the net result is that a used car will cost you about double the cash purchase price over five years.

Let's consider a four-year-old Toyota Camry LE, for example. In 2005 you could buy a 2001 Camry LE for about $12,251. According to Edmunds.com, the True Cost to Own that car over five years is actually $26,411. That's more than double the purchase price.

2001 TOYOTA CAMRY LE V6, PURCHASE PRICE: $12,251 TRUE COST TO OWN						
	YEAR 1	YEAR 2	YEAR 3	YEAR 4	YEAR 5	TOTAL
Depreciation	$1,443	$1,265	$1,114	$987	$886	$5,695
Financing	666	535	397	248	90	1,936
Insurance	820	849	879	910	942	4,400
Taxes & fees	791	51	51	51	51	995
Fuel	1,333	1,373	1,414	1,456	1,500	7,076
Maintenance	1,058	910	1,127	973	352	4,420
Repairs	225	328	380	442	514	1,889
Yearly totals	6,336	5,311	5,362	5,067	4,335	26,411

Source: Edmunds.com

So next time you're thinking about buying a car, new or used, take the cash purchase price and multiply it by two. Then seriously consider whether you're willing to spend all that money for something you may not really need. Bob Kurilko, a vice president at Edmunds.com, said some car buyers might find "they can afford to buy a car, but they can't afford to own it."

MORE TRUE-COST-TO-OWN EXAMPLES		
CAR MAKE AND MODEL	**CASH PURCHASE PRICE**	**FIVE-YEAR TRUE COST TO OWN**
2005 Suzuki Grand Vitara	$17,985	$36,767
2005 Ford Focus	$14,773	$29,043
2005 Nissan Sentra	$14,096	$28,310
2005 Volkswagen Beetle	$18,195	$29,566
2005 Chevrolet Cobalt	$17,914	$30,754
2005 Kia Sorento	$18,836	$38,136
2005 Ford Escape	$18,839	$33,075
2005 Honda Civic	$16,646	$26,608
2005 Toyota Corolla	$16,765	$27,527

Source: Edmunds.com

Why Do People Pay It?

At the risk of playing amateur psychiatrist, I often wonder why otherwise frugal people willingly spend so much money on their cars. I know people who are so thrifty they will not spend $5 on a Subway sandwich for lunch (choosing a 99-cent can of soup instead). Yet they drive a brand-new Ford Escape SUV. I suppose they rationalize this $600-per-month expense by telling themselves, "I need a car. How else would I get to work?" I also suspect they are unaware of what their car is *really* costing them.

Whatever the reason, it's time to look at the numbers for your particular situation. Because to make a good decision, you must use accurate data. So let's figure out what your car is really costing you.

CAR-FREE IN PITTSBURGH, PENNSYLVANIA

It seems that people often weigh the economic cost of transportation inconsistently. For example, I have heard people complain that the bus costs $2, but not complain about the enormous amounts of time and money they put into their car. I suppose $2 for the bus is cash, which one must physically hand over. A car, on the other hand, has many more hidden costs, which people seem to accept as a given without really questioning why they pay it. After living without a car you begin to see this. I guess my advice would be for people to weigh all the economic costs—time, money, aggravation, etc.—as fairly as possible.

—Jessi Berkelhammer, 28, graduate student

Figuring Out What Your Car Costs

The Edmunds.com True Cost to Own is a good start. And if you don't have time to run the calculations suggested in this section, the TCO will do in a pinch. But their calculations are based on estimating a limited number of variables. And their formula includes only certain categories of expenses.

The only way to really know what your car is costing you is to calculate it yourself. The following worksheet lists most of the expenses associated with car ownership. Please take your time filling in the blanks and try to think of all your car-related expenses. At the end we'll tally it all up and see how much of your hard-earned cash your car is consuming. You can also find this worksheet online at www.livecarfree.com.

It's best to run these numbers based on a full year, because you won't incur every expense in every month, and many will be lumped into certain times of the year. If you don't have actual receipts and hard data, it's okay to guess, but be as accurate as possible.

CAR COST WORKSHEET

Expense	Annual Cost
Total car payment *(x 12)* including sales tax	
Car payment late fees	
Total down payment divided by the number of years financed	
Other up-front dealer fees divided by the number of years financed *(destination charge, dealer prep fee, gas-guzzler tax, and so on)*	
Annual auto insurance premiums *(or monthly x 12)*	
Annual fuel cost	
Estimated annual depreciation*	
Annual state taxes/personal property tax	
Registration and license fees	
Emissions/environmental/smog test	
Repairs needed to pass smog test	
Car washes *(estimate based on number of car washes per month x 12)*	
Parking	
Monthly parking at work *(x 12)*	
Monthly parking at home *(x 12)*	
Parking at sporting events, concerts, etc.	
Airport parking	
Parking meters	
Valet parking at restaurants and clubs *(including tips)*	
Routine maintenance *(include all parts, labor, and tax)*	
Tune-ups	
Scheduled maintenance *(at mileage intervals)*	
Oil changes	
Transmission flush/lube	
Radiator/coolant flush	
Replace hoses and belts	
Replace windshield wiper blades	
Other routine maintenance	

Calculate depreciation by taking the price you paid for the car, then subtracting the car's current trade-in value, available at Kelley Blue Book online (www.kbb.com), then dividing by the number of years you have owned the car. Or use figures from Edmunds.com TCO tables. If you lease your car, please see page 26.

CAR COST WORKSHEET

Expense	Annual Cost
Mechanical and electrical repairs *(include all parts, labor, and tax)*	
New brakes	
Muffler	
Alternator	
Starter	
Fuel pump	
Headlights, fog lights	
Mirrors	
Air and fuel filters	
Radio antenna	
Other	
Body and cosmetic repairs *(door dings, dents and scratches, touch-up paint, windshield chips, hail damage, and so on)*	
Tires	
New tires (include all parts, labor, and tax)	
Cost to repair flat tire(s)	
Cost of clothing ruined while changing flat tire	
Towing fees	
Tire rotation	
Wheel alignment	
Snow tires and chains	
New battery	
Car products, accessories, and subscriptions	
Satellite radio installation, parts, and labor	
Satellite radio subscription *(monthly fees, taxes, and surcharges x 12)*	
On-Star or satellite navigation subscription *(fees and taxes x 12)*	
AAA *(American Automobile Association)* membership	
Car alarm installation, parts, and labor	
Radar detector	

CAR COST WORKSHEET

Expense	Annual Cost
Cell phone charger	
Cleaners *(e.g. Armor All, Windex, tire foam, wheel degreaser)*	
Car wax, cloths, buffers	
Gas tank additives	
Windshield washer fluid	
Ice scraper	
Car stereo, amplifier, CD player, car iPod adapter, stereo speakers *(include installation, parts, and labor)*	
Air purifier, air fresheners, fuzzy dice	
Tools, wrenches, etc.	
Repair manuals, do-it-yourself books, parts	
Jumper cables, de-icer, sand, salt	
Maps and map books	
Hub caps, wheel locks, alloy wheels	
Seat covers, steering-wheel wraps	
In-car organizers	
Window shades	
Window tinting	
Car covers	
License plate frames, decals, pin-striping	
Mud flaps, splash guards, running boards	
Interior floor mats	
Circuit breakers, fuses, and electrical connectors	
Tow hitch installation, hitch covers, and wiring	
In-car mobile phone installation and wiring	
Winter emergency kit	
Other car products	
Extended warranty cost *(divide total cost by number of years of warranty)*	

CAR COST WORKSHEET

Expense	Annual Cost
Parking tickets *(include late fees, doubled fines)*	
Speeding and traffic tickets *(include late fees, doubled fines, court costs, and any increase in insurance premiums)*	
Tickets for expired tags	
Towing and impound fees	
Traffic court fees	
DUI/DWI costs and fines	
Attorney fees	
Car theft/break-ins/vandalism *(estimate total cost)*	
Car crash costs and attorney fees *(include any increase in insurance premiums)*	
Medical bills from a car crash	
Lost work time and wages from car crash	
Property damage from a car crash	
Lawsuit from car crash *(estimate total cost)*	
Auto insurance deductible if you filed a claim	
Increase in premiums if you filed an insurance claim	
Locksmith fees for locking keys in car	
Cost to have new keys made	
Tolls	
Cost to have driveway shoveled after snowfall	
Cost for rock salt to spread on frozen driveway	
Cost to repair garage door that you drove into	
Cost to replace electric garage door opener	
TOTAL ANNUAL COST TO OWN YOUR CAR	
MONTHLY COST TO OWN (total divided by 12)	

Once you've calculated your total annual and monthly vehicle costs, examine the tables below. These tables will show you what the money you're now spending on a car would be worth if you saved it and invested it instead.

MONTHLY CAR COST INVESTED AT AN 8 PERCENT RETURN					
MONTHLY CAR COST	1-YEAR SAVINGS	2-YEAR SAVINGS	3-YEAR SAVINGS	5-YEAR SAVINGS	10-YEAR SAVINGS
$250	$3,112	$6,483	$10,133	$18,369	$45,736
350	4,357	9,076	14,187	25,716	64,031
450	5,602	11,670	18,241	33,064	82,325
550	6,847	14,263	22,294	40,412	100,620
650	8,092	16,856	26,348	47,759	118,914
750	9,337	19,450	30,401	55,107	137,209
850	10,582	22,043	34,455	62,455	155,504
950	11,827	24,636	38,508	69,803	173,798
1,050	13,072	27,229	42,562	77,150	192,093

If You Lease Your Car

If you lease your car you do not technically have depreciation, since you don't own the vehicle. However, you do have to give the car back at the end of the lease. This is essentially a balloon payment at the end of the loan. Additionally, all lease contracts require the lessee to pay a mileage overage fee for miles driven in excess of those allowed in the contract.

CAR-FREE IN OTTAWA, ONTARIO

Several years ago I came to a point financially where I could buy either a house or a car, but not both. I chose the house and never looked back. If you're a younger person who has bought into car culture and dreams of having a car, I recommend holding off on that because it's such a complete money drain. There are so many other opportunities open to you when you're not strapped to car payments.

—Lisa Routhier, 28

MONTHLY CAR COST INVESTED AT A 5 PERCENT RETURN					
MONTHLY CAR COST	1-YEAR SAVINGS	2-YEAR SAVINGS	3-YEAR SAVINGS	5-YEAR SAVINGS	10-YEAR SAVINGS
$250	$3,069	$6,297	$9,689	$17,005	$38,841
350	4,297	8,815	13,565	23,808	54,387
450	5,525	11,334	17,441	30,610	69,914
550	6,753	13,853	21,317	37,412	85,451
650	7,981	16,372	25,193	44,215	100,987
750	9,209	18,891	29,069	51,017	116,524
850	10,437	21,410	32,945	57,820	132,061
950	11,665	23,928	36,821	64,622	147,597
1,050	12,893	26,447	40,697	71,424	163,134

So when figuring the total annual cost to own your leased car, take the balloon payment amount (described as the "end of lease purchase price" in your contract), add any estimated mileage overage fees plus any turn-in fees at the end of the lease, then divide by the number of years in the lease. Write this amount in the "Depreciation" line in the Car Cost Worksheet.

Living Car-Free Is Not Free

Of course, living car-free doesn't mean you'll have no transportation expense. You will. But it will be a fraction of what you'd pay to own even the cheapest used car. For example, Anna Scalera lives

---

CAR-FREE IN CHICAGO, ILLINOIS

I'm sure we'd spend a lot more money if we had a car because it would be so easy to go to lots of stores and haul lots of stuff home in the trunk. Then we'd probably need a larger apartment! I've often noticed a phenomenon where I feel a desire to buy some shiny new product, but I don't get around to going to an out-of-the-way store to buy it for a while, and then I eventually lose interest in owning the product. Result: time, money, and storage space saved.

—Rochelle Cohen Lodder, 38, scientific copy editor

car-free in Portland, Oregon. She wrote me the following email itemizing her car-free transportation costs.

"My estimated annual expense for bicycling is around $150 per year. This includes a few tune-ups and occasional replacement of bike parts or lights. I occasionally take the MAX light rail train or the bus. Estimated annual expense for those fares is $28 ($1.40 x 20 trips). A few times a year when I really need a car I reserve a Flexcar. My estimated annual expense for car sharing is $90 ($9 per hour x 10 hours). Total: $268."

Your car-free transportation costs could be much higher, of course, depending on how far you live from work, how often you rent cars, ride mass transit, take taxis and airport shuttles, and so on. In many cities, a monthly transit pass costs around $55, or $660 per year. To get an accurate picture of how much money living car-free will save you, be sure to estimate your total annual car-free transportation cost, then subtract that from your expected savings.

CAR-FREE IN SAN FRANCISCO, CALIFORNIA

Although I could own a car, the financial drain would impact me in many ways. I lead a very busy, active lifestyle. I take frequent weekend trips—backpacking, cycling, road trips to other cities, etc.—all of which cost money. I also go out quite often—I enjoy SF's vibrant nightlife, and going out costs money. I enjoy going out to eat often at the thousands of great restaurants in SF, and going out to eat costs money. I travel to the East Coast a few times per year to visit family, which costs money. My point is, many of the things that I enjoy about my lifestyle cost money. I choose to spend my money in these ways, rather than pouring it into the cost of owning a car.

—Dustin White, 24, city planner

CHAPTER 3

The Quality-of-Life Costs of Owning a Car

"I know that some people count their car commute as free time, or time to unwind. That's bunk. During my free time I'm known to hit golf balls at the driving range, watch a movie, play cards, and even nod off. None of these things should be attempted while driving a car."

—TODD KOYM, CAR-FREE FOR EIGHT YEARS

This chapter is about *quality of life*, which is not the same as *standard of living*. A business executive who has a huge house, owns fancy cars, wears expensive suits, and eats in fine restaurants has a high standard of living. But if that same executive also has crippling debt, can barely make his mortgage payment, has high blood pressure and heart disease from lack of exercise, suffers from debilitating job stress, has no free time, and has anxiety about his personal finances, then he clearly has a low quality of life.

Living without a car can improve your quality of life. It can give you greater peace of mind, lower your stress level, improve your health, eliminate hassles, provide more social interaction, and maybe result in more free time.

Your standard of living can also improve. Without a car to pay for, you'll be able to buy a nicer house and have more money to furnish it. You may be able to afford real vacations and frequent dining out. The only part of the standard-of-living equation you won't have is the car.

Stop Hassling Me

An immediate benefit of going car-free is the long list of hassles and frustrations you'll eliminate from your daily routine. Every car—regardless of make, model, year, or price—comes with a collection of inconveniences and headaches that we wouldn't tolerate from anything else in our lives. Yet for some reason we accept this aggravation from our cars. By not owning a car, your exposure to these hassles, costs, and hazards will dramatically decrease, if not disappear altogether.

"Our life is frittered away by detail . . . simplify, simplify."

—Henry David Thoreau

THINGS YOU WON'T MISS ABOUT OWNING A CAR

- Rising gas prices
- Spending time at gas stations
- Sitting in rush-hour traffic
- Construction delays
- Wasting time looking for a parking spot
- Paying to park
- Remembering to feed your parking meter
- Mysterious engine noises
- Screeching brakes
- Interior squeaks and rattles
- Annoying minor repairs
- Costly major repairs
- Trying to find a reputable car repair shop
- Waiting for your car to be fixed
- Wondering if you were overcharged
- Hoping it's fixed right the first time

- Going back to have it fixed a second time
- Worrying about damage to your parked car
- Car theft, vandalism, and break-ins
- Chipped and cracked windshields
- Spending time and money on car washes
- Flat tires
- Paying automobile taxes
- Paying registration fees
- Dead batteries
- Scraping ice off a frozen windshield
- Waiting for the car to warm up on a winter morning
- Tailgaters
- Altercations with other drivers
- Road rage
- Waiting in line at the DMV
- Speeding tickets
- Parking tickets
- Tickets for expired tags
- Having your car towed and impounded
- Going to traffic court
- Waiting in line to get your oil changed
- Forgetting to bring the oil change coupon
- Rust and deterioration
- Shopping for a car
- High-pressure car salespeople
- Negotiating a fair price
- Worrying about paying too much
- Buyer's remorse

CAR-FREE IN ASHLAND, OREGON

The great payoffs are money and time. A car isn't just an expense—though my car-owning friends do seem to spend a huge amount of money on car payments, gas, repairs, insurance, etc.—it also eats time. After you go car-free, add it up and all of a sudden you may be surprised to find that you have time to have a life.

—John Michael Greer, 43, freelance writer

- Buying a lemon
- Manufacturer recalls
- Hail and storm damage
- Fender benders
- Driving over debris in the road
- Buying car-wash products
- Vacuuming the interior
- That feeling of dread when your car won't start
- Asking a stranger for a jump
- Shopping for car insurance
- Getting dropped by your insurance company
- Driving in snow and ice
- Uneven wear on tires
- Shopping for new tires
- Waiting to have tires rotated
- Trying to keep the mileage below the number allowed in your lease
- Paying a penalty for going over the allowed mileage
- Developing a sedentary lifestyle

Each of the items on this list, taken by itself, may not seem like a big deal. But what car owners fail to notice is the long-term, cumulative effect all these little nuisances have on overall quality of life. The items on this list cause aggravation, stress, and worry, and they contribute to a more complicated life. How nice it would be to leave all these problems behind. By going car-free you can.

CAR-FREE IN SYDNEY, NOVA SCOTIA

I don't have to worry about high gas prices. I don't have to worry about insurance. Plus, riding a bike has put me in better physical shape than I've ever been in my life. I've dropped over forty pounds and my blood sugar is entirely under control without medication (I am Type 2 diabetic). I've found that most people who *think* they couldn't live without a car only think that because they've used a car all their life and can't conceive of doing things any other way.

—John A. Ardelli, 33, quality assurance supervisor

FIVE MILES PER HOUR?

The typical American male devotes more than 1,600 hours a year to his car. He sits in it while it goes and while it stands idling. He parks it and searches for it. He earns the money to put down on it and to meet the monthly installments. He works to pay for petrol, tolls, insurance, taxes and tickets. He spends four of his sixteen waking hours on the road or gathering resources for it. And this figure does not take account of the time consumed by other activities dictated by transport: time spent in hospitals, traffic courts and garages; time spent watching automobile commercials or attending consumer education meetings to improve quality of the next buy. The model American puts in 1,600 hours to get 7,500 miles: less than five miles an hour.

—Ivan Illich, *Energy and Equity*

Time Is Money

The only thing cars soak up faster than your cash is your free time. Every item on the list above, every car wash and fill-up, every tune-up and oil change, every visit to the DMV, and every item you buy to keep your car running and looking good takes precious time. And that's just the beginning; you still have to include all the hours you spend actually driving your car.

According to the Surface Transportation Policy Project, the average American driver spends 443 hours behind the wheel each year. That's equivalent to eleven forty-hour work weeks, or one-fifth of an entire work year. Don't you have something else you'd rather be doing?

In a 2004 online poll, readers of Washingtonian *magazine voted overwhelmingly that commuting was their single largest waste of time.*

Depending on your particular situation, after you go car-free you may be surprised by how much more free time you have. It was one of the first things I noticed after getting rid of my car. And it was wonderful.

Of course, when you live car-free there will be delays and inconveniences that pop up in place of the many car-related time-wasters you'll be eliminating. For example, time spent waiting at transit stops and filling out rental car paperwork. But armed with the information and strategies in this book, your car-free lifestyle can be time-efficient and cost-effective. And every trade-off will be worth it tenfold.

Wasted Mental Energy

Cars also require our mental energy. Every year your car forces you to think through thousands of little scenarios. "Is it safe to park here?" "Should I fill up with gas now, or drive on and look for a lower price?" "What would happen if I didn't pay that parking ticket?"

A RIVER OF **TRAFFIC**
(AND ITS TRIBUTARIES)

When you don't have a car to worry about you'll have fewer decisions to make. Which means you can devote more mental energy to other endeavors, or just relax and give your brain a rest.

Traffic Congestion

Who wants to spend time sitting in traffic? Nobody. But when you own a car, traffic congestion is part of everyday life. According to a 2005 Federal Highway Administration study, the average American spends 51 hours each year sitting in bumper-to-bumper traffic. And traffic congestion is only going to get worse. In the year 2000 there were 215 million vehicles registered in the U.S. and 213 million licensed drivers. By 2010 there will be an estimated 262 million vehicles and 244 million licensed drivers.

Traffic congestion diminishes quality of life by keeping people from their family and friends and by preventing them from taking part in more productive activities

"Once we start widening roads to sixteen, seventeen, or eighteen lanes in each direction, that's when traffic will start running smoothly."

—Ellen DeGeneres, comedian

CAR-FREE IN SAN DIEGO, CALIFORNIA

Looking not too closely, someone might say that if I drove I'd have more time because it would take less time to drive. They'd be wrong when considering the time they spend feeding their car. Bicycling is the most efficient means of land travel known. That means it takes less time, effort, and cost to travel by bike. Therefore I have more time, energy, and funds for other things. Plus, some of my free/fun time *is* while biking to and from work. Yippee!

—Jim Baross, 59, management analyst

or recreation. Traffic jams also lead to a higher likelihood of car crashes, injuries, and death. Traffic congestion causes increased fuel consumption, engine emissions, and smog. And sitting in traffic can lead to stress, frustration, and road rage.

A 2005 study of urban traffic congestion by the Texas Transportation Institute estimated that traffic jams cause 3.7 billion hours of travel delays for U.S. drivers every year, and 8.7 billion liters of wasted fuel. The institute estimated the total cost of traffic congestion in the U.S. at $63 billion annually.

TRAFFIC ISLAND
(LOS ANGELES, CALIFORNIA)

WORST U.S. CITIES FOR TRAFFIC CONGESTION

Los Angeles, California
San Francisco, California
Washington, D.C.
Atlanta, Georgia
Houston, Texas
Dallas/Fort Worth, Texas
Chicago, Illinois

Source: Texas Transportation Institute, 2003

Health Concerns

Traffic jams can do more than just put you in a bad mood; they can ruin your health. According to Dr. Karol E. Watson, MD, PhD, director of the UCLA Center for Cholesterol and Hypertension Management, "Heavy traffic has been shown to produce a

THE AVERAGE AMERICAN WALKS JUST 300 YARDS PER DAY.

high degree of stress which could be a catalyst for stroke and heart attack. A stressful commute coupled with high blood pressure may be a dangerous combination for morning commuters." A study published in the October 21, 2004, edition of the *New England Journal of Medicine* supports that statement. The study concluded that sitting in traffic nearly triples the risk of suffering a heart attack a short time later.

The hallmark of car dependency is a sedentary lifestyle. A 2004 study by the RAND Corporation, the nation's largest independent health policy research organization, found that sedentary suburbanites are more likely to suffer chronic health problems such as high blood pressure, asthma, headaches, diabetes, migraines, urinary tract infections, back pain, and obesity. The co-author of the study, Dr. Deborah Cohen, said, "To improve our health the study suggests that we should build cities where people feel comfortable walking and are not so dependent on cars."

"Nowhere is there more temptation to eat junk than on the road."

—CBS Evening News, November 14, 2005

INTERIOR AIR QUALITY

But at least your car seals out the toxic exhaust emissions from other cars as you're driving down the highway, right? Wrong. A study by the California Air Resources Board found that exposure to air pollution may be up to ten times higher inside vehicles than in ambient air outside. Dr. Alan Lloyd, CARB chairman said, "We're learning that people's highest daily exposure to air pollutants may be during their commute to and from work." The study also concluded that engaging a car's air filtration system, or closing its air vents, did little to lower pollution levels inside the vehicle.

CRASH RISK

According to the National Highway Traffic Safety Administration there were 6.3 million motor vehicle crashes on U.S. roadways in 2003. Nearly 3 million people were injured in those crashes, and 42,643 people died.

Car crashes are the leading cause of death among children and young adults. U.S. Transportation Secretary Norman Mineta said the problem of highway deaths is a "national epidemic" and costs society $230 billion a year, or about $820 for every American citizen.

> *"Life happens between empty and full."*
>
> —AD COPY FROM A PHILLIPS 66 GASOLINE COMMERCIAL, OCTOBER 2005

CAR-LITE IN ST. LOUIS, MISSOURI

For as long as I can remember, my father would commute thirty to forty-five minutes each way to work. I remember him always complaining about the traffic and how it put him in a bad mood and made him cranky and tired. Sitting in his car for that long beat him up mentally. When you're tired from a day of work and a long commute, it's hard to muster up energy to do things with the family. So, from a young age I saw that sitting in traffic was less than desirable. Most people buy homes in the suburbs because they can get "more house for the money." However, what they're saving in house cost, they're almost spending in gas money and wear and tear on their car. So I moved to within one mile of work. I could go on for hours about the advantages. Like no longer having to plan my day around commuting and traffic, sleeping later, and having more free time. Now, I'm home in five minutes. It's so common for people to make excuses why they don't want to live closer to work. In my mind it's about quality of life, plain and simple. The less you sit in traffic, the better your life will be.

—Todd Schumacher, 30, play-by-play sports announcer

The Federal Highway Administration estimates the average total cost of a car crash with fatalities is $2.9 million. That cost includes: property damage, medical expenses, lost wages, emergency services, administrative and legal fees, travel delays, workplace costs, vocational rehabilitation, pain, and loss of quality of life. A nonfatal crash resulting in disabling injuries can cost nearly $1 million. The average cost of a car accident with minor injuries is $13,900.

Just watch your local news traffic report for a few days and you'll understand how common serious automobile crashes are. On any given day there are likely to be a half dozen accidents with injuries on your local news. The more you drive, the more likely you are to be involved in a crash.

"SHOULDN'T THEY WEAR HELMETS?"

CAR-FREE IN ANN ARBOR, MICHIGAN

There aren't many real dangers in modern life, but commuting at high speed on a congested highway is one. And it affects one's emotions; it is deadening and stressing. I could have improved my work situation had I commuted an hour in heavy traffic. I gave it thought but decided against.

—Tim Athan, PhD, 51, business development consultant

Road Rage

It is impossible to collect accurate statistical data on the number of road rage incidents. But a recent study of 11,120 drivers by the website www.roadragers.com found 38 percent of people admitted to getting into confrontations with other drivers. Seventy-eight percent admitted to using obscene gestures while driving. And 60 percent felt that "all other drivers are complete idiots." A survey conducted by the National Highway Traffic Safety Administration found 60 percent of people felt that unsafe driving by others is a major personal threat to their families.

"More than twice as many people have died since 1900 in U.S. car collisions as have been killed in all the wars in U.S. history. It is a heavy toll from a conflict largely overlooked: the war waged on us by the car."

—KATIE ALVORD, AUTHOR
OF *Divorce Your Car!*

So what leads to road rage? According to the NHTSA, "Many psychologists blame the intoxicating combination of power and anonymity provided by motor vehicles."

Noise Pollution

Automobiles are the primary source of noise pollution in cities. Noise pollution can cause sleep loss, headaches, stomachaches, increased blood pressure, degenerative hearing loss, and compromised immune system function. It can also have a damaging economic impact by lowering property values. Noise pollution makes conversation difficult and reduces human interaction.

A noise level of about 85 decibels can begin to cause hearing loss. A hair dryer typically runs at about 75 to 90 decibels. City automobile traffic ranges from about 80 to 100 decibels.

Animal Casualties

An estimated one million animals die on U.S. roadways every day. Automobiles harm wildlife in other ways, too. According to the

HIGHWAYS DIVIDE HABITATS

Humane Society, the most serious threat to wildlife in the U.S. is habitat fragmentation caused by road and highway construction. Fragmentation forces animals to live in areas too small to meet their basic needs for food, water, shelter, and finding a mate.

Sprawl

The Sierra Club defines sprawl as "irresponsible, poorly planned development that destroys green space, increases traffic, crowds schools, and drives up taxes." Suburban sprawl devours one million acres of forest, farmland, and open fields every year. Sprawl spreads out homes, schools, and amenities, which makes people drive more and spend more time in their cars and away from family. According to the Sierra Club, people who live in sprawling suburbs drive three or four times more than people who live in dense urban areas.

Sprawl is costly. Instead of spending money and tax dollars to improve existing communities, sprawl forces tax dollars to be spread thin building new roads and new schools and to fund new police and fire districts. And sprawl is self-perpetuating; more traffic leads to the widening of highways and new road construction, which in turn leads to more development, more cars, and ultimately more sprawl.

CAR-FREE IN CHAPEL HILL, NORTH CAROLINA
Overall, living car-free is easy. It just takes planning. I have a lot less stress in my life because I don't have a car. Driving is very frustrating. But for some reason people accept that. When I rent a car I'm reminded just how awful and nerve-racking it is to drive.

—James Coley, 47, university staff member

Why Pay All That Money for All Those Problems?

So basically, cars gobble our money, consume our time, squander our mental and physical energy, force us to sit in traffic jams, deteriorate our health, and cause us to risk serious injury and death every day. Why pay all that money for something that causes so many problems?

To be fair, when you live car-free you will incur some expense, some risk, and some waste, but only a fraction of what's created by owning a car. Learning to live without a car can not only change your financial life for the better—it can change your life for the better.

CAR-FREE IN LOS ANGELES, CALIFORNIA

I live in Los Angeles, California, where I'm the director of online sales for a small company. I've been completely car-free for five years. I made the choice foremost because owning a car is increasingly costly and frustrating—traffic congestion, taxes and fees, smog, parking. Plus, time spent in cars is of very low quality—because of social isolation, separation from the environment, and the low sensual quality of most road and highway infrastructure.

In stark contrast to that, living car-free is liberating, exhilarating, helps you meet more people, and creates greater social interaction. Life without a car is more varied, rich, and intense. And you have more sensory, intellectual, and social stimulation. You also stay thinner, look better, have a lower heart rate and higher endurance. I also eat better, fresher food because I shop at a local farmers' market. I find I can get 95 percent of everything I need within a short bicycle ride. If I wanted to, I could rent a car every weekend and still come out way ahead.

I have all the friends I did when I had a car, and new ones too. But unlike my friends who drive, I go to more places and do more stuff than anyone else I know because I never worry about parking problems.

Advice: just commit yourself to it and it becomes easy.

—Richard Risemberg, 52, director of online sales

CHAPTER 4

The Environmental Cost of Cars

*"We do not inherit the earth from our
parents, we borrow it from our children."*

—Antoine de Saint-Exupéry, author of *The Little Prince*

According to the U.S. Environmental Protection Agency, automobiles are the single largest cause of air pollution in this country, and driving a car is a typical citizen's most polluting daily activity.

But the negative effects of automobiles go far beyond smog. From mining raw materials, to the manufacturing process, and ultimately to the landfill, the automobile may be the single worst environmental catastrophe in human history. Here is a summary of the negative effects cars have on the environment.

Cars Devour Natural Resources

Nearly seventeen million new cars are sold in the United States each year. That's more than forty-five thousand every day, or one every two seconds. Automobile manufacturing is one of the largest industries in the United States.
It's also one of the most natural resource–intensive processes on the planet. Car manufacturing requires enormous amounts of steel, aluminum, copper, lead, nickel, zinc, plastic, and rubber. These natural resources must be mined, processed, and shipped at great expense to automobile factories all over the world.

Every car creates more pollution and material waste during its manufacture than in the entire time it's on the road. Steel production requires coal and limestone and results in sulfur dioxide, acids, and slag waste. Mining for zinc, copper, and aluminum destroys land, pollutes rivers and streams, and causes soil erosion.

The website www.environmentaldefense.org states, "The North American automobile industry is responsible for the release or transfer each year of more than 300 million pounds of lead through mining, smelting, manufacturing, recycling and disposing of lead-containing automotive components." Lead-based house paint was banned decades ago because of the serious risk even small amounts of lead pose to human health, especially to children.

"There are 850 million cars in the world today, and there'll be 1.1 billion in 2020. To put that in perspective, if you parked all those 850 million cars end to end around the equator, you'd need a highway 150 lanes wide."

—SCOTT FOSGARD, GENERAL MOTORS EXECUTIVE, AS QUOTED IN THE *Chicago Tribune*, FEBRUARY 10, 2006

Air Pollution

Every car exhaust pipe spews a toxic mixture of poisonous gases and particles into the air around us. These gases include carbon monoxide, hydrocarbons, sulfur dioxide, lead, and particulate matter. Cars are also the primary generators of greenhouse gases like carbon dioxide and nitrous oxide, which contribute to global warming.

CAR-FREE IN PORTLAND, OREGON

Driving is the new smoking. We all understand that driving wastes nonrenewable energy, pollutes, and contributes to unlivable and unsustainable communities through sprawl and traffic. We understand the dangers, but driving is so addictive we play down the effects. We complain, but we keep paying for gas, because apparently oil and all its associated costs, including human life, aren't high enough yet.

—Elisabeth Meyer, 22, college student

Studies show tailpipe exhaust from cars causes cancer, heart disease, respiratory illness, nervous system disorders, emphysema, and birth defects. When drivers fuel their cars at the gas pump, known carcinogens like benzene are released into the air. Exposure to benzene has been linked to a number of health problems, including increased risk of leukemia.

Automobile manufacturing plants also fill the air with poisons. Some of the byproducts of paints, epoxies, and solvents used in making cars include acetone, methyl chloroform, and xylene. The EPA says exposure to these and other air toxics may cause immune system disorders, reduced fertility, and developmental, reproductive, and respiratory problems.

Smog

Particulate matter from vehicle exhaust and tire erosion is the primary source of smog in many cities. Particulate matter refers to tiny particles of ash, dust, dirt, and smoke, combined with tiny droplets of liquid that may be composed of hundreds of different chemicals. Fine particles pose the greatest health risk since they can get into lungs and even into the bloodstream.

Particulate matter can cause chronic bronchitis, decreased lung function, respiratory illness, cardiac arrhythmia, and increased risk of heart attack. Particulate matter can also harm plants and animals by landing on soil and water and altering the nutrient and chemical balances of delicate ecosystems. Particulate matter can also cause damage, discoloration, and erosion to buildings, statues, and monuments.

Oil Consumption

The United States has less than 5 percent of the world's population but consumes 25 percent of the world's oil—twenty million barrels every day. More than half of our oil is imported. And according to the U.S. Department of Energy, two-thirds of U.S. oil consumption is for transportation. Locating and extracting oil causes water and air pollution, oil spills, wilderness and natural habitat loss, and violent armed conflicts around the globe.

Transporting oil wreaks havoc on the world's oceans. According to the National Academy of Sciences website, "About 210 million gallons of petroleum enter the sea each year from the extraction, transportation and consumption of crude oil and the products refined from it." Between 1973 and 1993, an estimated 200,000 oil spills took place in U.S. waters—an average of twenty-seven spills every day.

"We have to become independent from foreign sources of oil. We have got a serious problem and now's the time to fix it."

—President George W. Bush, on the CBS Evening News, January 28, 2006

In 1989, the *Exxon Valdez* tanker disaster spilled eleven million gallons of oil into Prince William Sound, Alaska, one of the worst spills in U.S. history. But the *Exxon Valdez* is not even among the top thirty largest oil spills. According to the Alaska Oil Spill Commission, oil discharges as big as the *Exxon Valdez* disaster happen somewhere in the world every year. Exxon repaired and renamed the *Exxon Valdez* and still uses it to ship oil today.

Only about 5 percent of oil pollution in oceans comes from major tanker spills, according to a traveling exhibit produced by the Smithsonian Institution. Every year, routine maintenance such as bilge pumping from ships of all types and accidental discharges from pipelines dump millions of gallons of oil into the world's oceans. More than twenty-two thousand miles of pipeline are used to transport oil in the United States.

Car Oil Changes and Runoff

The transport of oil is not the single biggest cause of oil pollution. Car owners improperly discard an estimated 240 million gallons of used motor oil each year—the equivalent of two *Exxon Valdez* spills per month. A typical car oil change results in five quarts of used engine oil, enough to contaminate one million gallons of fresh water. One quart of oil can create a two-acre oil slick. Yet 40 percent of discarded oil is dumped on the ground or down a sewer, 21 percent is thrown into the trash, and 6 percent is burned.

And millions of cars slowly leak oil. The Smithsonian Institution estimates that one year's worth of oil runoff from parking lots, paved surfaces, and roadways in a major U.S. city could contain as much oil as a large tanker spill.

> "A more fundamental problem with oil is that the cost to consumers of owning and operating a car does not reflect its full price to society. Drivers do not directly pay the monetary costs of global warming, air pollution, water pollution, and oil dependence."
>
> —THE UNION OF CONCERNED SCIENTISTS (WWW.UCSUSA.ORG)

Automobile Disposal

Cars are difficult to recycle because they contain dozens of different types of plastics and polyurethane, as well as lead, mercury, cadmium, zinc, oils, lubricants, cooling liquids, and sulfuric acid. Therefore nearly all motor vehicles are simply added to North American landfills and scrap yards—since 1946, an estimated 300 million of them. Eleven million cars are discarded each year, many simply abandoned.

According to the U.S. Environmental Protection Agency, Americans generated 290 million scrap car tires in 2003. Many end up in landfills and dumps. Fires at tire dumps pollute the air with toxic black smoke. One hundred million car batteries are also discarded every year.

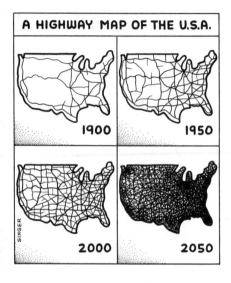

A HIGHWAY MAP OF THE U.S.A.

1900   1950

2000   2050

Road, Highway, and Parking Garage Construction

America's addiction to the car means a steady increase in the number of roads and highways, paved parking lots, tunnels, bridges, exit ramps, and multilevel parking garages. More paved surfaces mean less green space, fewer trees, and fewer parks. Widening roads to handle increased traffic often results in the removal of sidewalks and bike paths.

Building and maintaining car infrastructure comes with a tremendous price tag to taxpayers. According to Federal Highway Administration estimates, the average annual cost of U.S. highways and bridges will be $106.9 billion per year, every year through 2020.

Road, bridge, and parking garage construction harms the environment by depositing trash, paint, solvents, metals, grease, degreasers, oil, and other toxic chemicals into the soil. When rainwater filters through a construction site it can carry harmful pollutants into groundwater sources.

> *"Adding highway lanes to deal with traffic congestion is like loosening your belt to cure obesity."*
>
> —Lewis Mumford, sociologist and writer

Car-Free and Guilt-Free

Pretty much from the moment the first Model T rolled off Henry Ford's assembly line in 1908, the automobile has been an environmental debacle. So many problems, so few pages to write about them. If you want more background on how America was seduced and ultimately held hostage by the automobile, I highly recommend reading Katie Alvord's excellent book *Divorce Your Car!*

The good news is that we don't have to be part of the problem. Most people have no idea how much damage cars cause. Now you know. And helping the environment is just one more reason to seriously consider going car-free. Wouldn't it be great to be car-free, debt-free, and *guilt-free*?

CAR-FREE IN PORTLAND, OREGON

When the oil runs out, car-free living will really gain popularity, or finally car manufacturers will notice that gas-guzzlers aren't going to be the most lucrative choice on the lot and will be motivated to develop and market alternatives on a large scale. Alternatives to this country's car-centered lifestyle aren't a pipe dream, they are imminent.

—Amy Potthast, 32, manager of a nonprofit

CAR-FREE IN PROVO, UTAH

I live car-free for several reasons: (I) to do my part in helping reduce greenhouse gas emissions and other environmental pollutants; (2) to help wean our nation from foreign energy sources; (3) I like riding my bike and it keeps me in shape a whole lot better than having an internal combustion engine do all the work for me; (4) car usage encourages sprawl development; (5) traffic congestion and the "need" to expand our roadways is very costly, and I'd rather be part of the solution than part of the problem; (6) driving causes otherwise nice people to get road rage—I've yet to get road rage on my bike or on the bus; (7) the average American family spends between $6,000 and $8,000 a year on car-related expenses and there are other things I'd much rather spend my money on than a depreciating pile of metal.

—Travis Jensen, 29, engineer

CHAPTER 5

But Can You Really Live without a Car?

"If you live in a city, you don't need to own a car."

—William Clay Ford Jr., CEO of Ford Motor Company
(quoted in *The Observer*, November 12, 2000)

As you learned in the previous four chapters, there are many compelling reasons *not* to own a car. So then why do so many Americans have one? Or more to the point, why do we feel like we need one? There are two reasons: one simple, one insidious.

Our Self-Perpetuating Car Culture

Owning a car seems like a normal life necessity because most of us literally grew up in cars. After we were born, our first experience outside the hospital was riding home in a car. We were raised in two-car families. We spent our formative years comfortably cocooned in car seats. As children we ate and napped in cars. We

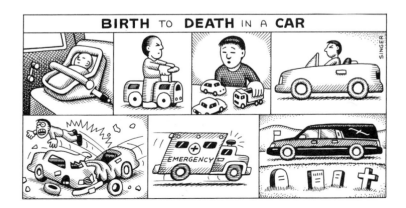

BIRTH to **DEATH** in a **CAR**

watched our parents drive to work, to the bank, to the gas station, and to the drive-thru, and basically spend much of their lives behind the wheel.

As teenagers, most of us gradually joined the car culture our parents, purposefully or unknowingly, instilled in us. We eagerly anticipated getting a driver's license. Then we drove to proms, practices, jobs, and college in cars. So it's no surprise that when we became adults we blindly followed the example set by our parents. When we got our first job, we applied for a loan and went into debt to buy our first car.

From birth, cars are as much a part of daily existence for most of us as eating and sleeping. It's no wonder most Americans don't question why or even whether they need a car—they just accept it as a necessary part of life.

Advertising: A Powerful Force

The second reason millions of Americans feel a natural, almost innate need to own a car is the aggressive advertising and marketing done by the automobile and oil industries. Studies indicate that citizens of the United States see as many as three thousand advertisements each day. That's about one every twenty seconds. And nearly 20 percent of those are car or car-related advertisements.

The auto industry buys more advertising than any other business in the world. Advertising spending on cars, trucks, SUVs, and related products exceeds $20 billion annually. Three of the six largest advertisers in the U.S. are automakers.

And there's no question automobile ads are effective. Car companies employ the brightest creative minds on Madison Avenue to craft ad campaigns that work on both conscious and subconscious

CAR-FREE IN CHICAGO, ILLINOIS

Advertisers and automakers have spent the better part of a century telling us that cars are a symbol of freedom. So it's hard for people to see that they're much more free when they get rid of their car.

—Ted Ernst, 34, social services administrator

levels. Occasionally car ads tout the features of certain models. But most automobile advertising promises the intangibles: image, status, sex appeal, fulfillment, and freedom. Car ads show attractive young people (actors) in sporty coupes zipping along empty roads smiling and having a good time. They never show cars stuck in traffic, in line at the gas pump, polluting the air, or mangled in fiery crashes.

Automakers, oil companies, and the advertising industry have been playing on the same powerful team virtually since the automobile was invented. That's nearly a hundred years and hundreds of billions of dollars spent with one goal in mind—to make every adult in America think he or she needs a car. As the saying goes, if you say something loud enough and long enough, people will start to believe it.

MISLEADING ADVERTISING FOSTERS CAR ADDICTION

When I was trying to find a publisher for this book, one skeptical editor said to me, "Chris, I don't think people will give up their cars, because people in this country *love* their cars." Not only is that a sweeping generalization of two hundred million car owners, it's also untrue for most of them.

CAR-FREE IN SALT LAKE CITY, UTAH

Years of car advertising promise that if you own the right car, it will fill all the voids in your life. One thing many of these ads emphasize is the safety factor: "Own our car, and it will keep you and your children safe." It's an outright lie, and they ought not to be allowed to say it. If you think about it, the same misleading techniques were used to advertise cigarettes until just a few years ago.

—Michael Wise, programmer-analyst

There certainly is a small percentage of people who truly love cars. These are the folks who read car magazines, watch automobile television shows, and wash their car twice a week. The extreme ones even enjoy changing their own oil—good times! Yes, it would be fair to say that these people "love" their cars.

But the vast majority of car owners in this country do not have a *love affair* with their car—they have an *addiction* to it. And like any addiction, it's a costly one. Most Americans spend their entire adult lives feeding this addiction with precious time and money simply because they don't know any other way; they don't know there is a viable alternative to a car-based existence.

> "Most of the luxuries and many of the so-called comforts of life are not only not indispensable, but positive hindrances to the elevation of mankind."
>
> —HENRY DAVID THOREAU

But here's the good news. First, in most cases all it takes to cure car addiction is a little information and some mild lifestyle reengineering. As Katie Alvord writes in her book *Divorce Your Car!*, "Auto dependency is a psychological addiction, not a physical one." And second, it's never too late to change your ways and get on the car-free path to personal and financial freedom.

CAR-FREE IN DAVIS, CALIFORNIA

National transportation policy, especially since World War II, has effectively been controlled by General Motors, Exxon, and their associates. These corporations have used their considerable political influence to ensure that highways get funded and transit systems don't, creating an extensive system of subsidies to encourage driving cars and discourage alternatives. The automobile-centered U.S. transportation system has been created to maximize profits, not to enhance personal mobility.

—Paul Dorn, bicycle activist

Alternatives to Owning a Car

Shifting from car-dependency to a car-free or car-lite lifestyle does require making some adjustments. If you're a car owner, you may be used to operating under the if-I-want-to-go-anywhere-I-have-to-drive mentality. The rest of this book is designed to open up new ways of thinking about transportation.

Believe it or not, more than twenty million Americans commute to work using modes of transportation other than a car that they own. According to the 2000 U.S. Census:

- 6,592,000 people commute to work each day by public transit
- 14,300,000 people carpool to work each day
- 3,417,000 people walk to work each day
- 158,000 people commute by motorcycle each day
- 2.8 million people occasionally commute by bicycle
- 567,000 people regularly commute by bicycle
- 4,075,000 people work at home and do not commute at all

As more people become frustrated by rising gas prices, growing traffic jams, and the ever-increasing cost of owning a vehicle, the number of car-free commuters is increasing. According to a study by the Center for Transportation Excellence, public transportation ridership increased 22 percent from 1998 to 2004.

CAR-FREE IN PHILADELPHIA, PENNSYLVANIA

Though the automobile is widely advertised as necessary to adulthood, success, freedom, and sex appeal, I've found this to be an illusion. There's a cost to living outside the box. But there's a greater cost to living inside it.

—Paul Glover, 58, consultant

The Six Keys to Car-Free Living

There are six main criteria that determine whether you are a good candidate for car-free or car-lite living. If you answer yes to most of the following questions you should have an easy time transitioning to a car-free or car-lite lifestyle. If you say yes to only three out of the six, we'll show you strategies to overcome the sticky spots. And even if you answer no to every question, don't worry, there's still hope—but you will have to make some substantial changes, such as where you live.

1. CAN YOU GET OVER YOUR OWN EGO?

Honestly, this is the toughest one for most people. The auto industry has done a fabulous job of convincing Americans that their status and self-worth are tied to their cars. So it's perfectly natural for you to wonder, "Will people think I'm a loser if I don't drive a car?"

I can tell you from personal experience, when you don't own a car people do not assume you are financially unsuccessful; rather, they view you as unusual, independent, and interesting. Most people admire those who are committed to their own values. Plus, any anxiety you have about status will quickly evaporate when you see your bank account grow by thousands of dollars every year.

CAR-FREE IN CHICAGO, ILLINOIS

I've been car-free for three years. I think the hardest part of making the decision to go car-free is bridging the "I can do it" gap. In other words, most people have bought into the advertising message that cars are necessary and bikes are only for fun. Getting over that mind-set is more difficult than actually living without a car. You'll be surprised how easy car-free life is once you try it. The concept can be intimidating at first, but you'll quickly get over it. It's a confidence thing. There is a learning curve for the typical car-reliant person, but nothing insurmountable.

—Todd Gee, 34, computer programmer

2. CAN YOU GET TO WORK RELIABLY WITHOUT A CAR?

If you can get from your home to your place of employment and back safely and on time without a car, then you probably don't need to own one. Virtually all other errands and outings—such as grocery shopping, post office, the mall, dinner with friends—are trips you can accomplish without driving.

At this point some lifelong car owners might be tempted to throw their hands up and say, "The *only* way I can get to work is to drive." But before you make such a definitive declaration, keep one thing in mind: car owners often don't even notice alternative forms of transportation in their own neighborhoods. So even if you're absolutely convinced that driving a car is the only way you can commute to work, don't despair. I'm willing to bet we'll have that problem solved for you by the time you're halfway through this book.

3. DO YOU LIVE IN AN URBAN AREA, OR IN A MIXED-USE DEVELOPMENT?

People who live in or near cities will find it much easier to get around without a car. Cities have more transportation options, better pedestrian infrastructure, easier access to facilities, closer proximity to services and attractions, and housing is more concentrated than in rural communities. All these things make cities ideal for car-free living.

CAR-FREE IN BOISE, IDAHO

My bike commute is frequently the best part of my day. I feel great when I get to work. I feel great when I'm riding. I feel great when I get home. Win-win-win.

I hear a lot of excuses—people telling me why they are bound to their cars. I, too, could rationalize that if I wanted to. I'm a middle-aged fat guy. But I've ridden a bike to work—and for essentially *all* my local transportation—for twenty-plus years. I live four miles from work for a reason.

If you want to live fifty miles from the office on "Heaven's half-acre" and commute to work every day, I support your right to make that choice. But you must weigh the consequences of that choice.

—Steve Hulme, 51, computer programmer

I'm not suggesting you need to live in downtown Chicago. Many smaller towns have everything you need to live car-free. And developers are now doing a much better job of creating mixed-use developments where schools, shopping, entertainment, and recreational facilities are built in among the new homes.

If you live in suburbia or out in the country, you may have to make some significant changes before you can live car-free. But all is not lost. Keep reading.

4. DO YOU HAVE ACCESS TO PUBLIC TRANSPORTATION?

According to the 2000 U.S. Census, 49 percent of Americans live near a transit stop. If you live within one mile of a bus line or subway stop you're golden. One mile is an easy, healthy walk. Plus, many bus lines these days are equipped with exterior bike racks. So even if you live several miles away, you can pedal your bike to the bus stop, then load your cycle and hop on board. If you're unfamiliar with the mass transit system in your area, we'll help you figure it out in chapter 10.

5. DO YOU LIVE IN CLOSE PROXIMITY TO AMENITIES?

It helps a lot if you live within a few miles of the amenities that are important to you. For me these include my health club, my church, a public library, parks and green space, a local market, bars and nightclubs, a FedEx Kinko's location, and sports stadiums. I've managed to find a place to live within one mile or less of all those things. You will have to determine which amenities are essential to your lifestyle.

CAR-FREE IN JEROME, ARIZONA

You don't need to be in a big city to live without a car. I have lived car-free in Seattle, Washington; Thousand Oaks, California; Arcosanti, Arizona; and even the hill town of Jerome, Arizona. I love walking to nearby restaurants, to the theatre, and around the community.

—Randall Hunt, hospitality worker

CAR-FREE IN NEWPORT BEACH, CALIFORNIA

I'm the senior network engineer at the University of California, Irvine. I'm also a single parent and a homeowner in Newport Beach, one of the most affluent communities in the country. There are various auto dealerships in Newport Beach including Rolls Royce, Mercedes, Jaguar, Range Rover, and Ferrari. Here I am, living amongst an auto culture living auto-free.

In Southern California everything is centered around the car. Given this, it's still easy to live auto-free. I am able to get around by bicycle and public transportation with little effort. I see plays, films, concerts, and attend lectures. My commute to work is on a bicycle and I love it. Four of the seven miles of that commute is along a bike path adjacent to natural wetlands. Here, I don't see any cars at all. There are many subtle pleasures of a car-free lifestyle.

—Mike Scott, network engineer

6. ARE YOU FLEXIBLE?

Being willing to make changes and adapt to new situations is an important requirement. Because when you live car-free or car-lite, you often replace old ways of doing things with new ways. If you deplore change of any kind, then perhaps the car-free lifestyle isn't for you.

What About Families with Children?

Singles or couples *without* children will find it easiest to live car-free. The typical suburban "soccer mom" who spends much of her life in a minivan driving four kids to practice, games, piano lessons, and birthday parties will find it difficult to live without a car. But it's certainly not impossible, especially if your children are old enough to bicycle or if you have car sharing in your community.

CAR-FREE IN TORONTO, ONTARIO

My husband and I live car-free in Toronto. It has allowed us to purchase a home and build up equity. The hardest part of living car-free is being bombarded by automobile advertising, which leads to constant pressure to conform and drive like everybody else.

—Ryan Lanyon, 29

If you're a parent with children and you've answered yes to most of the six criteria above, you have an excellent chance of living car-free. But first, skip ahead to chapter 28, which provides advice for multiple-car families. Perhaps that's a better place for you to start.

Can *You* Live Car-Free?

If you've read this far without slam-dunking this book into the circular file (or worse yet, searching for the receipt to return it), chances are good that you are an excellent candidate for either living car-free or reducing your car use and living car-lite. Millions of Americans are already doing it. And tens of millions of Americans can do it if they want to. I'm quite confident that includes you.

CAR-FREE IN WASHINGTON, D.C.

I live in Washington, D.C., and get around by walking, Metro, and bus. I walk to and from work (about three miles round trip). All the car ads on television promote the idea that cars are synonymous with freedom. For me, *not* having a car is the real ticket to freedom—not getting stuck in traffic, not driving around for hours trying to find a parking spot, not worrying about having one's car broken into, no insurance or high fuel prices to pay, no stress at the DMV, etc. In addition to these psychological, time, and financial benefits, not having a car is good for my health and the environment. I get valuable exercise walking to work, to the store, to meetings. And I'm not emitting climate-changing gases into the air.

—Anna White, 31, nonprofit manager

CHAPTER 6

From Car-Dependent to Car-Free:
My Story

> *"Don't even consider keeping up
> with the Joneses. They're broke!"*
>
> —DAVE RAMSEY, BEST-SELLING AUTHOR OF
> *The Total Money Makeover*

The point of this chapter is to demonstrate that almost anyone—from corporate executives to bar and restaurant workers—can go from driving fifteen thousand miles a year to seldom driving at all, and be happier, healthier, and *much* wealthier. I'm living proof that even hard-core car addicts can change their ways—to the enormous benefit of their bank account and their quality of life. Here's my story.

Who Is Chris Balish?

I am as mainstream as you can get. I work a nine-to-five job in an office building. I commute to work. I wear conservative clothing. I go out on dates. I go to bars, sporting events, parties, concerts, and festivals. I eat meat. I don't buy hemp or tofu, and I don't live in a commune. In fact, I live in a sweet two-story loft in a trendy part of St. Louis, which I can easily afford because I don't have to pay for a car.

Image Is Everything . . . or Is It?

Let's go back a few years. In 2002 I was driving a shiny new $36,000 SUV. It was a dark blue Toyota Sequoia with a big V8 engine, power everything, and enough seats to fit all my friends. I loved that thing, and I kept it immaculate. It was expensive, but

I thought my status as a TV news anchorman necessitated an impressive ride and a flashy image. So I paid the price. Although I didn't know how dearly I was paying at the time, because I never sat down to run the numbers. What was important to me was that I looked good and everyone thought I was successful.

I was driving about fifteen thousand miles a year back then. I drove to work, to the grocery store, to the mall, to the dry cleaner, to the gym, and about twice a week to the gas station. Whenever I needed *anything*, I just hopped in the SUV. Sale on shoes at the mall? Off I'd go—whether I needed shoes or not. Late-night craving for chocolate chip ice cream? Hand me the keys and get out of my way. Met a cute girl who lives forty miles away? Hey, that's what cars are for, right?

This lifestyle didn't seem wasteful or extravagant to me at the time, because all my friends behaved the same way. It wasn't unusual for one of my buddies to make three separate trips to Home Depot in a single day. Another friend would drive to the gym in the morning to do his cardio routine, then drive back to the same gym at night to lift weights. And the gym was less than a mile away.

Whatever whim we had could be satisfied by driving somewhere. It was the life we lived because

> *"It is possible to have too much of a good thing."*
>
> —AESOP (c. 620–560 B.C.E.)

it was the only life we knew; each of us was the product of a car-centered, suburban upbringing. No doubt about it, we were hard-core *autoholics*. And we were just like most of America, addicted to our cars out of habit.

The Truth Hurts

So there I was, rolling up to clubs and parties in my pride and joy, my main image-maker and status symbol—my car. It reflected the flashy façade I was trying hard to maintain—that I was successful and raking in the cash.

But that image was a lie. I did have a comfortable income. But like so many other Americans, I was spending it as fast as it came in (a little faster, actually). It appeared to all of my friends and girlfriends that I was living the good life and rolling in the dough. But on the inside, I was stressed out and worried about my financial future. I knew I had to find some way to radically improve my personal finances; I just didn't know how.

Accidentally Car-Free

Every time gas prices shot up, I felt acute pain in my wallet. So I decided to sell my large SUV and buy a new car, something smaller and more fuel efficient, but still sexy and impressive. So I ran a classified ad in the local newspaper. I predicted it would take at least a month to find a buyer, so I had not even begun to shop for a new car.

Needless to say I was astonished when the very first person who came to look at my Sequoia purchased it on the spot. He gave me a cash deposit that day, and a cashier's check for the remaining amount the next day. I was glad the sale went smoothly. But for the first time in my adult life I was without a car. And I was *terrified*! How would I get to work? How would I get to the mall? What would become of me!

Luckily I sold the Sequoia on a Friday, so I had all weekend to figure out how I was going to get to work on Monday. But it didn't take all weekend; it took about twenty minutes. I got on the computer and typed the words "public transit" and "St. Louis" into

CAR-FREE IN BERKELEY, CALIFORNIA

I only work thirty hours per week in a very expensive place to live in large part because I don't have a car and don't have to pay for insurance, gas, maintenance, tolls, parking, etc. I couldn't do it if I owned a car. I think people don't realize how much cars actually cost in terms of both money and the time spent earning the money.

—Sean Brient, 43, drafter

the Google search engine. The first website that came up was www
.metrostlouis.org. So I clicked on it and was taken to the home
page of the mass transit system for the greater St. Louis area. Then
I clicked on the System Map tab. A few minutes later I located
a transit stop about half a mile from my house. I was surprised,
because I didn't even know that stop was there, even though I'd
driven by it hundreds of times. I guess I never looked.

Since I had not ridden the Metro system in St. Louis before
(or anywhere else for that matter), I was nervous about it. So on
Sunday, I went for a trial run to see if I could get to work this
way. Sure enough, it was simple, easy, convenient, air-conditioned,
clean, safe, and on time. Plus, I brought a newspaper with me and
read it during the trip. I was amazed at how well this worked.

Learning to Live without a Car

Over the next few weeks I rode the Metro to work every day. It
took a little getting used to for a die-hard car addict like myself.
But I didn't have a single problem and I was never late to work.
As a bonus, my commute was now productive time—I could
read, write, or work on a laptop computer. Plus, I didn't have to
sit in bumper-to-bumper traffic on a crowded expressway breath-
ing exhaust fumes with stressed-out drivers road-raging at me. I
thought, "This is not a bad way to get to work. I could easily do
this for a month or two until I buy a new car."

What I had to figure out next was my non-work-related transportation. How was I going to get to the gym, to the mall, to the
grocery store, to the post office, and all the other places I was used
to driving in my car? And what about going out to bars and parties

LOTTO MILLIONAIRE DOESN'T OWN A CAR

Garry McGivney won the second largest New York Lotto jackpot ever on July
29, 2005. According to WROC-TV news, the NBC television affiliate in Rochester,
despite his $56 million windfall, "This millionaire doesn't even have a car. The
retired 66-year-old state worker says he loves to walk and would probably just
rent a car if he ever needed one."

with my friends? I was afraid that my social life was about to come to a screeching halt, and that I would starve to death because I couldn't get to the grocery store.

I soon realized that all the little errands I used to run by driving around town and burning up gas, could easily be accomplished without ever setting foot in a car. I found a grocery store that delivers right to my doorstep. I started buying stamps and clothing by mail order. I found a neighborhood fitness club three blocks from my house. And I began doing all my banking online and at ATMs. I even found a website that rents movies and DVDs by mail.

My Social Life

Now this part may be a little hard for you to believe, but it's true. After I sold my car, my social life actually *improved*. I was afraid that without wheels I'd be sitting home alone on Saturday nights eating bonbons on the couch, instead of out having fun with my friends. It turns out that getting rid of my car resulted in my being *more* social and spending *more* time with my friends, not less.

Here's why. When I had a car and I needed to go somewhere— say to the mall or to Sam's Club—I just drove there when it was convenient for me, usually right after work. This meant I would drive there alone, shop alone, and drive home alone. Plus I was driving to and from work alone. Being car-dependent is a solitary existence in many ways.

But after selling the car, trips to the mall or to Sam's Club became group outings. My friends knew I didn't have a car, so they'd say,

CAR-FREE IN PITTSBURGH, PENNSYLVANIA

When I tell people I live car-free most are somewhat incredulous—especially here in Pittsburgh. It's such a car-centric town. But more people than I would have expected express a degree of envy that I live without a car. A lot of people tell me they can't do it because they're not fit enough, or because of where they live. So I've often biked to their houses on a route they often drive, just to prove it's possible. Anyone can try the car-free lifestyle.

—Jonathan Mayes, 25, Pittsburgh Symphony administrator

"Dude, I'm going shopping on Saturday, you wanna go?" They drove, I treated them to lunch, we spent time together, it was perfect.

Going to sporting events, parties, bars, and nightclubs was also easy. Most places I could get to on my own via the Metro. Or I would take a taxi, ride my bike, or just plan outings closer to home.

This was an eye-opening period for me. I couldn't believe nearly a month had passed since I sold my car, yet I was still getting all my errands done and going to all the places I wanted to go. I was as socially active as ever, even though I didn't have a car. For the first time in my life the thought occurred to me, "Do I really even *need* a car?"

The End-of-the-Month Shocker

Of course, thirty years of brainwashing by automobile advertising still had a firm grip on my inner psyche. Secretly I was enjoying this car-free experiment. But outwardly I told all my friends I was still shopping for a car. And, truth is, every time I saw a sexy sports car zooming down a deserted highway in a TV commercial, I felt the lure of car ownership beckon.

Then my entire outlook on cars changed in a single moment. I was checking my bank balance online—as I did frequently in those days—when I saw a mistake on the computer screen. That couldn't be right. How much? How could that possibly be? And there's no minus sign in front of that balance.

I was so busy figuring out this living-without-a-car thing that I'd completely forgotten: no car payment this month. Not to mention no car insurance premium, no $40 fuel tank to fill every week, no $9 car washes, no $30 oil changes, no monthly parking fee, no Armor All or wheel cleaner to buy, and no parking tickets. My bank balance was $800 higher than usual at the end of the month. It was like Christmas!

Doing the Math I'd Never Done

The first thing I did was balance my checkbook, to make sure there was no mistake. Then I examined my bank and credit card statements from the past several months. Sure enough, the $800 that now resided in my bank account was the same amount I had been spending on my car every month.

I realized a universal truth: every car—from luxury sedan to subcompact, new or used—comes bundled with dozens of different expenses that siphon cash from your wallet faster than you can say "late fee." The care and feeding of an automobile is far more costly than I ever realized. I was actually angry with myself for never sitting down before this to figure out how much money I was spending on my car.

That $800 windfall got me thinking. I wondered how much money I had spent on cars in the past ten years. I estimated that since college I had blown at least $70,000 on cars. If I had invested that money instead, and earned a return of 8 percent, I would have $106,000 in the bank.

Well, no use beating myself up over things I can't change. So I decided to look to the future. I calculated that if I stayed car-free for a year it would be the equivalent of getting a $13,000 annual salary increase. I could pay off my credit card balances, establish a rainy day fund, and start saving to buy a house. And if I decided to remain car-free permanently, I could pay off the mortgage and retire twenty years early. Hmmmmm . . .

Benefits beyond the Financial

Needless to say, after looking at the hard numbers I decided to stretch out this no-car thing as long as possible. I still thought that I'd end up buying a car eventually, but hey, why not rake in some easy cash for a few months?

As I continued to ride the Metro around town and spend more time with my friends, little light bulbs kept turning on in my mind to illuminate even more benefits of car-free living. I noticed that I had more free time. I found it easier to relax. And I was no longer staying late at the office because I was getting work done *during* my commute.

With so many advantages to not owning a car, I kept postponing the purchase of a new one. Until one day I realized, *I don't want to own another car*. What I learned through this experience is that when you live car-free not only do you save a ton of cash, but also your quality of life improves. It's a win-win. And for me it was a no-brainer.

My Life Now

Since I gave up owning a car I am now totally debt-free, I'm saving an amazing 50 percent of my income, and I'm on track to retire at age forty-five. Plus I live a more fulfilling life. And I still get everywhere I need to go with ease.

I am living proof that a busy professional with a nine-to-five job really can go from driving fifteen thousand miles per year to rarely driving at all, and be much happier. Not to mention a heck of a lot richer.

CHAPTER 7

Okay, but I'm Still Not Ready to Give Up My Car

"Living without a car is a tremendous luxury. Most people who are car dependent can't understand that, but it is."

—MEGHAN BURKE, CAR-FREE PhD STUDENT

You've seen how cars pollute our air and water, cause social and health problems, waste time and energy, and cost a fortune. But you may still be having a hard time visualizing your life without a car. Or maybe you're actually *afraid* of being without a car, since you've probably owned one all of your adult life.

Well, don't freak out; there's no need to make any decisions just yet. We still have a lot to cover before you have all the information you need to make the choice that's right for you. It's perfectly natural to fear the unknown. So in this chapter we'll look at some of the most common fears associated with giving up one's car.

Fear of Becoming Isolated, Cut Off, or Stranded

If you've relied on cars for transportation your whole life, the thought of no longer having one may cause worry. "Will I ever see my friends again?" "Will I become a recluse?" "Will I die alone?" Relax. Your life will be better without a car, and that includes your social life.

Contrary to what you might think, you're not going to be stuck at home on Saturday nights just because you don't have a car. Many people find that after they adopt a car-free lifestyle they spend more time out and about, and more time visiting and socializing. When you don't own a car you'll meet new people and develop new relationships because you'll be carpooling and sharing rides more. You'll get to know other residents in your community because you'll no longer be zooming through it at forty miles per hour insulated by glass and steel. And you'll meet neighbors when you're walking down the street or riding your bike.

If you follow the advice in this book, you won't be cut off from other people or from the things you want to do, and you'll never get stranded. You will, however, have to reengineer your transportation and plan things in advance. The remaining chapters of this book will help you with that reengineering process.

Fear of Being Too Limited

Will not having a car limit the things you can do? Well, yes and no. The cost savings of living car-free provide tremendous freedom. In many cases, people who don't own cars live lifestyles more rich and varied than people who do. However, living car-free can make it more difficult to go where you want exactly *when* you want.

When you have a car you can drive anyplace at any time. Printer out of paper? Let's go to OfficeMax right now. A light bulb just burned out? Hop in the car and head to Home Depot. Craving Taco Bell? Grab your coat. A car is instant, on-demand transportation—but at a tremendous cost.

When you don't own a car, you will lose some of your ability to make instantaneous travel decisions. If a trip involves traveling outside the area you can easily get to by bicycle or mass transit, the

CAR-FREE IN PORTLAND, OREGON

I was apprehensive about living without a car. How, for example, would I visit my parents? Leave town for daytrips to the Columbia Gorge where I love to hike? How would I get to church on Sunday morning? I feared that giving up my car, even temporarily, would strip me of independence. As it turned out, I made my parents come see *me*, found places to hike closer to home, and started going to a closer church service by bike and now by carpooling. Cars are awesome tools. They just aren't necessities for most people who live in a metropolitan area.

—Elisabeth Meyer, 22, college student

errand may have to wait until another day. So you may not be able to replace that light bulb *right now*, but you will be able to replace it. Without a car you learn to plan ahead, to be patient, and to delay instant gratification.

Fear of Peer Pressure

I have found that many people in this country have bought into the marketing myth that every adult in America must own a car. And when they meet someone who does not own a car they think it's peculiar. You need to accept this fact before making the decision to live car-free.

Fortunately, this odd form of peer pressure is mild and usually comes in the form of sincere questions. "Do you *really* not have a car?" "How can you live without a car?" "How do you buy groceries?" "But everyone has a car."

In most cases, people who ask are genuinely interested in your answer. They're not poking fun. They're intrigued, because they realize on some level that they are car-dependent themselves.

Of course, a guaranteed way to avoid such questions would be to follow the pack and own a car. But remember, the average American credit card balance is over $8,000, seventy-two million credit card holders make only the minimum payment each month, and an estimated nine million Americans seek credit counseling every year. So if you want to follow the pack and be like everyone else, go into debt and buy a car.

CAR-FREE IN BELLINGHAM, WASHINGTON

A car is a big thing to have to take care of, and not having to do so lightens my load. I feel really rich now that I don't have a car to support. I seem to have more free time, and greater peace of mind. I get just as much done, without too much running around all over town. I seek out fun places, stores, and restaurants within a mile of my house, and surprisingly, there are plenty.

—Carol Berry, 48

Fear of Criticism and Jokes

"Hey, Chris. When you go out on a date this weekend, are you gonna pick her up on your bicycle?" Ha ha. In my years of car-free living I've been the butt of a few jokes. Some of them are quite funny. All are harmless. And since I've heard them all before, I know how to respond. For example, I usually reply to the joke above by saying, "No. Actually with all the money I'm saving by not owning a car, we're flying to Cancun for the weekend." Another effective comeback is, "What's the price of gas these days? I have no idea."

I've also noticed that the people who seem to crack the most jokes are usually the ones who are stuck with an expensive car and a huge car payment. My guess is that they secretly envy my smart financial move and that's why they make jokes.

Fear of Losing Your Identity, Image, or Status

When I was researching this book, a man said in an interview, "Going car-free seems to have a lot of benefits, and I could definitely use the extra cash. But I don't want to give up a possession that reflects who I am. My car helps me express my identity and status."

This is a common psychological objection to giving up one's car—even though most people would never admit it. The fact is

---

CAR-FREE IN MILWAUKEE, WISCONSIN

I spent about $4,000 a year on a leased vehicle. I felt that was a lot of working hours just keeping the car available to me on a moment's notice. I realized I could do it cheaper even if I rented a car two weekends a month.

—Bill Sell, 67, business owner

no one buys a Porsche because the top speed is 150 miles per hour. They buy it for status and image.

The short answer to the above objection is that when you live car-free you'll find better ways to express your individuality. With the time and money you'll be saving, there are hundreds of opportunities for creative new forms of self-expression.

For example, instead of spending your money on a sports car, you could take an art class and fill your home with canvases that *you* painted. Or you could buy a fancy digital camera and become a photography hobbyist. Or maybe you'll use the money you're not spending on a car to take a year off and travel the world.

There are far better ways to present a successful, interesting image than by owning a car. Besides, even if you drive a bright red BMW convertible, there are still hundreds of other people in

CAR-FREE IN SEATTLE, WASHINGTON

My husband and I have not owned a car for the last four years. We decided to get rid of the car for economic reasons—we did the math and it just didn't make financial sense. When we sold the car, I must admit I had a twinge of panic as it was being driven away. But we never missed it. Being car-free is great. We are making more friends in our neighborhood and community, shopping at more local stores, and dealing with less noise, pollution, traffic congestion, and parking hassles. Environmentally, we are using less oil, emitting less noxious fumes into the air, and creating less waste. So there are many levels of benefits.

We recently bought a house and could afford a better location since we are spared the care and feeding of several automobiles. We walk to the store or ride our bikes together. We don't have to join a gym or make any conscious effort to get exercise since our active transportation modes keep us moving. It's much easier to get yourself to walk and bike places if you don't have a car sitting right there.

Advice to people: add up the actual costs of car ownership. Include gas, car price, insurance, oil changes, parking fees, cleaning, and repairs. It's much higher than most people think. Also consider your time—driving is quick but parking might not be, and repairs, fueling, etc., all take time. Then add in the other time it takes to get exercise. People who own cars also tend to offset the speed advantage of a car by shopping less efficiently, living farther away from work, etc. Consider these all as part of the choices you make.

—Emily Allen, 35, consultant

your city with the *exact same car*. So really, a car doesn't make you unique at all. If you're a person who only derives your identity and self-worth from the car you drive, then my guess is you probably stopped reading this book long ago.

Consider It an Experiment

Here are two final, comforting thoughts for those of you who are still skeptical. First, if you're not convinced you want to give up your car *entirely*, you can use the strategies in this book to gradually *reduce* your car use. Second, even if you take the plunge and sell your car, only to realize later that this lifestyle doesn't suit you, you can always just buy another car. It really is that simple and that easy to end your car-free experiment. In the meantime you will have saved some money and learned a lot about yourself.

So what have you got to lose?

PART TWO

Getting to Work without a Car

CHAPTER 8

Car-Free Commuting:
It's Easier Than You Think

> *"Self-reliance is the only road to
> true freedom, and being one's own
> person is its ultimate reward."*
>
> —PATRICIA SAMPSON, WRITER

Being able to get to and from work reliably is a fundamental requirement for living car-free. Clearly, if you can't get to your job on time every day, you've got problems. The next six chapters will help you do that. Not only will you be able to get to work reliably, you'll also find your car-free commute more enjoyable and more productive. At the end of this chapter we'll even reveal a system

"I BOUGHT A HOUSE IN THE COUNTRY FOR SPACE AND QUIET,
YOU KNOW? ONLY NOW I'M IN THE CAR IN HONKING
GRIDLOCK TRAFFIC OVER HALF MY LIFE ..."

that will virtually guarantee you'll never miss a day of work because you don't have a car.

Researching Transportation Options

What would you do if gas prices shot up to $5 per gallon? (Which, incidentally, may happen not too far in the future.) You'd probably start looking really hard for a way to get to work that didn't involve driving your car. Could you ride the bus? Take the train? Carpool? Ride your bicycle? These are the questions to ask yourself in this chapter. Is your car truly necessary, or is it just a convenient habit?

> **TOP TEN CITIES FOR CAR-FREE COMMUTING**
> 1. Boston, Massachusetts
> 2. Chicago, Illinois
> 3. Denver, Colorado
> 4. New York, New York
> 5. Philadelphia, Pennsylvania
> 6. Portland, Oregon
> 7. San Diego, California
> 8. San Francisco, California
> 9. Seattle, Washington
> 10. Washington, D.C.
> *Source: Kathryn Keller, Women's Sports & Fitness magazine*

Researching transportation alternatives is simple and easy and won't take much time at all. Half the battle is just opening your eyes to what's around you. Here are the best ways to find a car-free route to work.

EXPLORE YOUR NEIGHBORHOOD AND COMMUNITY

If you currently have a car, take a drive around the neighborhood where you live. Look for things like bike paths, bus stops, sidewalks, light rail lines, hotels with taxi stands, pedestrian overpasses, park-and-ride lots, car-sharing hubs, rental-car company locations, shuttle and trolley stops, and carpool or vanpool sites. Make a note of what you find. We'll show you what to do with the information later.

TALK TO FRIENDS AND NEIGHBORS

You might be surprised to learn that your next-door neighbor or a friend from down the street takes the bus or rides his bike to work. But you may never know unless you ask. Finding someone on your street or block who can show you the ropes is one of the best ways to learn about car-free commuting.

Also look for bicyclists, motorcyclists, scooter riders, walkers, joggers, in-line skaters, and other people moving around your neighborhood without a car. Stop and ask them where they're headed and how they get to work and back. Most people who don't rely on a car for their daily needs are proud of that fact and eager to talk about it.

ASK YOUR COWORKERS

People you work with are a good source of car-free commuting information because they go to the same place you do every day. If you have an internal email system, send out a mass email asking to hear from car-free commuters. Or post a flyer on a company bulletin board or on the refrigerator in the lunchroom. Chances are good you'll find a few people who don't drive to work. Ask them for advice and suggestions.

CONTACT YOUR LOCAL MASS TRANSIT AUTHORITY

Most cities have some sort of bus, train, or other public transit system. One of the most important parts of a successful mass transit program is providing useful information to users. A simple phone call to your local transit authority can usually provide you with a system map, user's guide, and a brochure with commuting tips. Another option is to visit a transit stop and talk with other riders about their experiences.

SEARCH THE INTERNET

One of the many blessings of the information superhighway is that it can help us stay off of the asphalt highway. Just go to www .google.com and type in your city name, the plus sign (+), and the words "public transit" in quotation marks. For example, when I do this for the city where I live, I type "St. Louis"+"public transit" and press Enter. Then just peruse the results.

You'll probably find the official website of the public transit authority in your city, plus other groups and organizations that promote the use of mass transit. You may find it beneficial to repeat the search using your city plus the words "mass transit." Sometimes these terms provide different results.

Most mass transit providers have excellent, user-friendly websites. Your first stop should be the system map. You'll be able to see right away if a bus line or light rail stop is located near your home or office. Most public transit websites also have tips for new riders, fare structures, monthly pass information, and a list of rules and prohibited items.

CONTACT LOCAL GROUPS

Almost every city has a group that advocates living car-free. Many of these are local chapters of national organizations. These groups are easy to find by doing a Google search with the keywords "car-free"+"[your city]."

There are also bicycling, walking, motorcycling, and scooter clubs in almost every city. These organizations are an excellent source of information for commuting without a car. Most bicycle shops can get you in touch with other bicycle commuters.

VISIT CARPOOLING WEBSITES AND MESSAGE BOARDS

As the cost of owning a car continues to escalate every year, so does the interest in carpooling. If two people are going from the same neighborhood to the same office building, why shouldn't they ride together and split the costs?

CAR-FREE IN BROOKLINE, MASSACHUSETTS

I believe that nearly anyone can live car-free; however, it requires some careful choices. One is to live near your work site. Another is to live near public transportation. A third is to understand that living car-free doesn't mean that you *never* use a car; just rent one when you want to go someplace outside the Hub.

—Thomas John Vitolo, 27, research assistant

National websites have sprung up to connect carpoolers. Visit www.erideshare.com and you can browse the carpools available in your area. The website also links carpoolers for running errands and for out-of-town travel. We'll cover carpooling in more detail in chapter 11.

CALL YOUR LOCAL CHAMBER OF COMMERCE

If you're still striking out, you may want to call your local chamber of commerce. Efficient transportation is vital to the economic success of any city. And the chamber will be able to get you in touch with public transit organizations. Most chambers also have some sort of welcome kit, which they will mail to you. These kits usually include maps, coupons, and information about local attractions, as well as a list of regional transportation providers.

Taking Notes and Brainstorming

Now don't go making any decisions just yet about which form of transportation suits you best. There's a lot of important information in the following chapters that may change your thinking. For now, just gather information: talk to people, get to know your neighborhood, surf the web, and jot down notes as you go.

CAR-FREE IN PORTLAND, OREGON

Although I initially decided to lose the car to save money, that isn't nearly as big of a concern for me today. I make approximately $70,000 a year, and my spouse makes about $30,000 a year. Rather, the biggest benefit for me is that not owning a car is just *easier*.

When we looked at buying a home last summer, before looking at anything I plotted the public transportation route to downtown. It had to be one mode only (i.e., no bus or train transfers), and it had to be less than thirty minutes, which is the longest commute I was willing to do. It ended up leading us to a condominium right next to the MAX light rail train. Not taking care of a yard fits the stress-free attitude that being car-free has given me.

—David Dyk, 23

This is also a good time to do some alternative transportation brainstorming. Take a sheet of blank paper and jot down all the ideas you have about getting to work without a car. Don't worry if an idea seems too outlandish or goofy. Sometimes those silly ideas lead to something viable later on.

Combining Modes of Transportation

While you're in this information-gathering phase it's important to remember that you can combine modes of transportation to meet your needs. For example, the solution that ultimately works best for you may involve riding your bicycle two miles to a transit stop, then taking the bus or train from there. Keep this in mind as you research various alternatives.

Triple Redundancy

Here is a strategy that virtually guarantees reliable car-free commuting. Triple redundancy means that in addition to your primary mode of transportation to work, you also have two backup modes. So if for some reason you can't get to work the normal way, you

CAR-FREE IN RENO, NEVADA

I've lived car-free for nearly ten years now in my hometown of Reno, Nevada. The most powerful motivation was a financial one. After my first two years of living car-free, I calculated that I had saved somewhere around $8,000 by ditching my old 1979 Toyota Celica (which I paid cash for). This enabled me to finance my first trips to Europe—the first four years it was for one month or so, the fifth year, for four months. And in 1998, when I was only twenty-four years old, I bought my first home—thanks in great part to the extra cash I had in the bank.

The biggest challenge of living car-free is the reorganization of one's life that is necessary in order to live without a car in an American city, which is basically planned around automobiles. This might mean moving closer to where you work, learning and adapting to the public transport schedules, or exploring your town for the best bicycle routes. In the beginning it's hardest, but I found the challenge fun and it has proved to be very rewarding.

—Peter Menchetti, small business owner

have something to fall back on. A system of triple redundancy gives car-free commuters confidence that they can get to work on time every day.

Here's an example of triple redundancy. I normally commute by riding my bicycle to work. I know that eventually I'll probably get a flat tire or have some other mechanical malfunction. It hasn't happened yet, knock on wood. But one time there was an ice storm and the roads were too slick to cycle. My primary backup was to call a coworker who drives past my neighborhood on his way to work. I have his cell phone number with me at all times. So if I need a ride, I can call him and ask for a lift. If he goes out of his way to pick me up, I'll usually buy him lunch that day—a small price to pay for the one or two times a year I need him. If that coworker is on vacation or I can't reach him, I can fall back on my second backup, walking to work.

Here are some more examples of triple redundancy:

PRIMARY MODE	SECONDARY MODE	EMERGENCY BACKUP
Carpool	Bus	Bicycle
Scooter	Bicycle	Walk
Commuter rail	Bus	Motorcycle
Bicycle	Ride with coworker	Work from home

Be sure to think about triple redundancy as you do your research. The key is to have backups arranged ahead of time, so you know exactly what to do if you're forced to go to plan B. You may never need your backups, but having them will give you the peace of mind to get rid of your car without worrying about getting to work.

In reality, this system of triple redundancy could accurately be called quadruple redundancy. Because a fourth option—albeit an expensive one—is to call a taxi. In my years of car-free commuting I have yet to call a taxi to get to work.

CHAPTER 9

Should You Move Closer to Where You Work?

"I have little sympathy for people who complain about long car commutes because they have the power to change their situation and choose not to."

—JON HILL, CAR-FREE BICYCLE COMMUTER

Let's say you've followed all the steps in the previous chapter, you've scoured the Internet, you've talked to your neighbors, you've done all the research, but you still can't find a viable car-free way to get to work. Perhaps your home is in the suburbs and there's no mass transit where you live and you can't find a carpool. The million-dollar question is: should you pack up and move closer to where you work?

The Million-Dollar Question

If you remember the savings chart from chapter 1, you know this really could be a $1,000,000 question. Investing the money you'll

CAR-FREE IN WASHINGTON, D.C.

People tell me I'm lucky to live in a location so convenient to everything I need. I tell them luck had nothing to do with it. I made a deliberate decision. You have the power to choose where you live, where you work, and how you get around. Because I don't have a car to pay for, I have a nicer home in a more convenient location—two miles from work. And I have more money in my retirement account. Just think of what you can do with $500 per month. When you take into account that money has been taxed, it's like getting a $9,000 raise!

—Todd Koym, 37, foundation program officer

save by living car-free for thirty years could be worth a million bucks. So if moving to a new apartment or house closer to work and/or closer to a mass transit stop is the only way you can live car-free, I suggest you seriously consider it.

I've devoted a separate chapter to this question for two reasons. First, I know this difficult dilemma will apply to many readers. And second, I feel so strongly about the benefits of living close to work that I want to emphasize the point. This is the only time in this book you will see a sentence in bold, all-capital letters: **LIVING WITHIN A FEW MILES OF WHERE YOU WORK WILL CHANGE YOUR LIFE**.

Of course, choosing to move close to where you work only makes sense if you plan to stay in the same job, or work in the same area. These days few people spend their entire careers working for the same employer. But then again, few people spend thirty years living in the same house or apartment. According to the U.S. Census, Americans move an average of twelve times in their lifetime. So why not coordinate the two? If you feel your job is reasonably secure and you're not planning to jump ship anytime soon, this strategy can really pay off. In fact, even if you do plan to look for a new job eventually, a few years of a micro-commute can be well worth the cost of a move. Factor in these considerations as you weigh your options.

CAR-FREE IN ITHACA, NEW YORK

Right now, we live two and a half blocks from my place of work. So convenient! I love having the ability to go home for a freshly prepared lunch and sometimes a siesta (as an Italian-American, very important to me). I can also run home if I forget a book, my cell phone, or anything else I may need throughout the day, which is extremely convenient. Also, by choosing to live downtown, we situated ourselves within walking distance of the things we use: library, restaurants, movie theaters, etc. If we lived out in the 'burbs, we would need to drive to these places. We are average citizens who have seen a better way to live, and are living the better way.

—Nicole Tedesco, 23, urban planner

More Free Time

The closer you live to work, the more free time you'll have. For example, if you currently live fifteen miles from where you work, you probably spend about forty-five minutes commuting through rush-hour traffic by car. A forty-five-minute commute each way means you're spending seven and a half hours a week—375 hours a year—driving to and from work. That's the equivalent of nine full work weeks behind the wheel.

If you moved to an apartment, loft, house, or condo within one mile of where you work, you could bicycle to the office in about five minutes (averaging twelve miles per hour). That would knock your commute time down to ten minutes a day, fifty minutes a week, and just over forty hours per year. You would realize a time savings of six and a half hours a week, or eight full work weeks annually.

Those numbers may be a bit hard to get your mind around, so think of it this way. How would your life improve if you had an extra six hours of leisure time every week? You could spend six more hours with your family. You could spend an hour a day at the gym. You could train for a marathon. Write a book. Take a cooking class. Learn to play piano or guitar. Or get an extra hour of sleep every night. The possibilities are endless.

CAR-FREE IN SAN LUIS OBISPO, CALIFORNIA

I highly recommend that anyone who is renting and commuting more than twenty minutes to work should relocate closer to their place of employment. Rent might be cheaper in the suburbs, but that difference is quickly lost in the cost of the commute.

If you decide to move, look for good cycling routes to your destination (bike paths, bike lanes). If you rent an apartment where carrying your bike up and down three flights of stairs every day is the only answer, so be it. But try to find a ground-floor apartment or an apartment building with a garage and a bike rack. Also try to find a place close to the bank, post office, grocery store, and a transit stop.

—Barry Lewis, librarian

CAR-FREE IN BERKELEY, CALIFORNIA

My wife and I moved from Davis to Berkeley, California, a couple of years ago, motivated in part by a desire to drive less. For years, traffic congestion has ranked as the number-one problem in annual surveys of San Francisco Bay Area residents. Accordingly, location was at the top of the list of our house-hunting criteria, specifically proximity to public transit and a diverse commercial district. We eventually bought a lovely home next to a park only two blocks from BART (the regional subway), three to six blocks from two major shopping streets, a three-minute bike ride from downtown, and a ten-minute bike ride to the Capital Corridor regional commuter rail that goes to Davis and Sacramento (frequent destinations for us).

Our car use plummeted, because we make essentially all of our everyday trips by foot, bike, or BART. We sold one of the two cars, and kept the other for weekend trips to the mountains and occasional work-related trips I make to out-of-town destinations. The remaining car was totaled by a snowplow a couple months later (the car was empty in a parking lot at the time). We took this as a divine sign that we should go ahead and make the leap into the terrifying unknown of car-free living!

We have now been car-free for seven months, and it has proved easier and considerably less expensive than we expected. We love it! Here are some details about our strategy and experience that might be useful to others:

- We shop close to home. We have no desire to drive twenty miles to a big mall to choose from a selection of a hundred brands of toothpaste! If we can't find something within bike/BART distance, we buy it over the Internet.

- For trips to out-of-town destinations that require a car, we first try to carpool with someone else [who owns a car] going on the same trip (e.g., a business meeting or ski outing). It is surprising how often carpooling is possible if you just call a few people and ask to ride with them. If that doesn't pan out, we borrow or rent a car. In the last seven months, we have rented cars about four times.

- Driving is remarkably habitual. Once you settle into a habit, it appears to be the only way to do things. But now that we have switched to a walk/bike/BART lifestyle, it no longer even occurs to us to use a car for local trips. And what's all the whining about being too old or out of shape to bike, or that biking isn't safe? That's just a rationalization to avoid having to think about your life and actually implement changes to improve it. The driving-

TV-couch potato-overweight-out-of-shape downward spiral leads to self-fulfilling whining and negativism. It's not as if you have to be a college-aged jock to ride a bike. My wife and I are forty-nine years old and work long hours at desk jobs, and biking's no problem. It's just a matter of what you get used to.

- When I'm on a bike, I never get stuck in traffic and I always get a front-row parking space. Whenever I'm driving, it seems I'm always stuck in congestion.

- Specifically, focus on location, location, location. If you can't switch your job to somewhere near your home, then move to a residence that's close to your work or to a transit line that goes to your work. If it's raining, wear a raincoat or get a little wet—it's no big deal. Attitude is everything. If you decide it's possible to live without a car, it will be.

—Gus Yates, 49

More Benefits of a Micro-Commute

If you live within a mile or two of work you could walk, jog, in-line skate, or ride a bike to the office. You could go home for lunch or to take a midday nap. You wouldn't have to pay for mass transit or wait at the bus stop. You could sleep later because your commute only takes a few minutes. After work you'll be relaxing at home before your coworkers even get to the highway entrance ramp. And you'll get regular daily exercise *during your commute*. So you can lose weight, firm up those thighs, burn more calories, look better, and feel better without ever going to the gym. Plus you'll save money.

And, of course, if you move to a home within a mile or two of work, getting rid of your car practically becomes a no-brainer. When you're close enough to walk or bike to the office, your need for a car will plummet. And after you ditch the car, you'll have plenty of extra money to buy that home gym, guitar, or piano, or to take that cooking class.

CAR-FREE IN BERKELEY, CALIFORNIA

I am so happily car-free you wouldn't believe it. Alternative transportation is something every city and county offers to some degree. And it helps to be in the right place to maximize safe transport and time savings by close proximity. Changing jobs and residences to conform to transportation considerations can mean an improved lifestyle. Choose to live where non-car living is supported, such as easy access to services via walking, close proximity to transit, and bike paths and bike lanes. Then get a good bike that doesn't look so fancy it will be stolen.

—Jan Lundberg, publisher

Corollary: Get a Job Closer to Home

If you can't move to a new home closer to your job, consider getting a new job closer to your home. Obviously, this is a very personal decision that depends on many factors. But it's easier to do than you might think. Visit local businesses in the area and ask for applications. Or identify the key employers within a few miles of your home, then do an internet search to find their websites. Most companies post current job openings online.

Changing jobs may seem like a big step, and it is. But it's a move that could mean hundreds of thousands of dollars to you over your career.

The Next Best Thing

Of course, not everyone can live within a few miles of their workplace. So the next best thing is to find a home near a major transit

CAR-FREE IN VICTORIA, BRITISH COLUMBIA

Many people try to live in the suburbs and, hence, have to commute an hour each way. This is two hours of their life taken away, for which they are not paid, nor compensated for their transportation costs. I can get to work in fifteen minutes by bike at very little cost (bike maintenance) and I maintain my fitness level at the same time. From a numbers perspective, this has got to be a no-brainer decision. I would never work for a company I couldn't reach by bicycle easily.

—Eric Davies, 42, computer programmer

stop or bus line. This will still allow you to get rid of your car and enjoy all the benefits of car-free living.

Doing the Math

Some simple math will help you with the decision of whether or not to move to a new home. Estimate your total cost to move—including moving expenses, realtor fees, penalties for breaking your lease, and so on. Then divide that total by the monthly cost of owning your car, which you calculated in chapter 2. This will give you a good estimate of how many months it will take to pay for the cost of moving. Be sure to factor into the equation any increase in rent or mortgage payment in the new location, and the cost of a monthly transit pass and possibly the purchase of a bicycle.

Remember that once you break even, you'll be car-free and watching your bank account swell every month thereafter. You can read more about the benefits of living close to where you work in chapter 14.

CAR-LITE IN CARLSBAD, CALIFORNIA

We move around a lot because of my husband's career. Part of our decision-making process of whether to take a new job or not is whether we can live in a place where he could bike to work. And if we can easily access other amenities by biking or walking. Only if the answer is "yes" would we take the new job. Then we look for a place on a bike path near the amenities we want.

In my case, I look for jobs after we're already settled. So I only job hunt at places I know I can get to by bicycle. I wouldn't even bother applying for a job at a place that would require a long car commute. It does limit my employment options, but I know the car commute would have such a negative impact on my life, that it's a trade-off I'm perfectly willing to make.

—Holly Ordway, 30, college English teacher

CHAPTER 10

Mass Transit

> *"If you think about it, some of the most meaningless times in life are spent in a car."*

—JIM VIEHMAN, JOURNALIST AND CAR OWNER

If you want to avoid high gas prices and minimize the stress of commuting, then let someone else do the driving for you. Mass transit comes in many forms—bus, train, subway, ferry, light rail, heavy rail—and it has considerable advantages over driving your own car. Most cities in the United States have some form of public transit system. Larger cities have any number of modes of mass transit. So chances are good that your city has an efficient and cost-effective way to get you where you need to go.

Don't Be a Transit Snob

Unfortunately, many car owners are "transit snobs." You know the type. People who say things like, "I wouldn't be caught dead riding

CAR-FREE IN ASHLAND, OREGON

The best way to size up a potential area is to go there and walk around. Look for parks, stores, restaurants, nightlife spots; your goal is to find a home close enough to the other places you want to spend your time that everything is within walking distance. If you're new to car-free living or don't know the area, rent, don't buy. Functional public transit is a necessity. This doesn't require a big city; some small towns have surprisingly very workable bus service. Map out the routes on a city map; you'll save yourself a huge amount of commuting time if you live close to a route that will get you directly to work, without having to transfer from one route to another.

—John Michael Greer, 43, freelance writer

the bus." That's too bad, because mass transit has come a long way in recent years. Public transportation is a $32 billion industry that employs 350,000 workers. According to the Center for Transportation Excellence, the average income of rail commuters in the U.S. is $50,000. And according to the United Transportation Union, thirteen million Americans ride public transit every day.

There are lots of reasons why so many people use public transportation. First, it costs just a fraction of what driving a car costs. Second, it eliminates many of the hassles of commuting by car. And third, the brightest minds in engineering, architecture, design, and urban planning have spent decades researching the best ways to move people around cities. The fruits of their research are modern mass transit systems that are:

- User-friendly
- Safe
- Clean
- Reliable
- Heated and air-conditioned
- Dry and sheltered from the weather
- Efficient

CAR-FREE IN SANTA ROSA, CALIFORNIA

Seven years ago my commute to work was about forty miles each way. I did this for three years, until it didn't matter how much I was getting paid, it wasn't worth the horrible traffic, not to mention the stress, and hardly ever getting to see my husband. Now my office is a mile from my house. It is really nice to have to make the decision each morning of "should I do the fifteen-minute walk, or the five-minute bike ride?" With our house being close to public transit and working close to home, I found after a few months my car was not getting driven but maybe once or twice a month, yet I was still paying my monthly car payment and my insurance. So, I decided to sell my car. I have been car-free for nine months now! That's like losing a couple thousand pounds!

—Christine Culver, executive director of Sonoma
County Bike Coalition (www.bikesonoma.org)

Not only that, but mass transit systems are designed to:
- Go to the most popular places, like sports stadiums, arenas, shopping centers, and hospitals
- Run with greater frequency during peak hours
- Run at convenient times
- Connect to other forms of transportation, like airports

Mass transit also helps alleviate traffic congestion, which is one of the primary barriers to economic growth in cities around the country. Efficient public transportation helps attract new businesses, major conventions, and national sporting events. It also provides mobility for seniors and the disabled.

Panhandling and soliciting are strictly prohibited on virtually all forms of public transportation.

IT'S FASTER THAN YOU THINK

"Riding the bus takes too long." This is a common misperception about mass transit. But when you factor in all the time needed to keep a car clean, fueled, maintained, and parked, commuting by mass transit may actually come out ahead. For example, when you take the bus or train to work, you don't have to drive to the top of a multilevel garage looking for a parking spot. You don't have to leave work every two hours to feed a parking meter. You don't have to stop at a service station to fill up

CAR-FREE IN SANTA ANA, CALIFORNIA

As our freeways become more clogged, many commuters realize the benefits of taking the bus, commuter rail, and subway. In Southern California, often the commute time is equal to or shorter than by car. I utilize transit agencies in five counties to go wherever I want, without the hassles that car drivers deal with. I carry around a book, or newspaper, or headphone radio to pass the time.
—Kiril Kundurazieff, 45, the Cycling Dude (www.cyclingdude.com)

with gas. You don't have to wait for your car to warm up on a cold morning, or scrape ice off your windshield. And rail commuters never get bogged down in rush-hour traffic jams.

IT'S LESS STRESSFUL

The beauty of letting someone else drive is that you get to sit back and relax. You don't have to worry about tailgaters, bad drivers, cars cutting you off, or drivers slamming on their brakes in front of you. And you'll never get road rage or be a victim of it. Heck, you can even take a nap.

TRANSIT TIME IS PRODUCTIVE TIME

When you drive a car to work, you have to concentrate on the road and on the other drivers around you. So multitasking is at a minimum. At most, you can talk on your cell phone or listen to the radio.

But when you let someone else drive, you can actually make your commute a productive part of your day. You can read the newspaper, catch up on magazines that have been piling up, work on a laptop computer, watch a DVD, write letters, memos, or email, prepare for a presentation, read a book, or study for a graduate degree. I keep a manila file folder in my backpack labeled "Metro Reading." Whenever I come across something that I'd like to read but don't have time to during the day, I throw it in that file and read it on the train.

CAR-FREE IN SACRAMENTO, CALIFORNIA

There's certainly a lot more variety in the people I meet on the train than in my regular circle of friends and acquaintances. It's taught me to have fewer preconceptions and to listen better. Most of the people on the train are just regular people. I admit that I tend to look down my nose at people who aren't imaginative enough to try getting out of their cars and taking a different and more interesting route to work.

—Owen Howlett, 31, energy efficiency researcher

SAFER THAN DRIVING

Riding a bus is about eighty times safer than traveling by car. Taking the train or light rail is forty times safer than driving. And, yes, these figures take into account that many more people drive every day than use public transportation. According to the National Safety Council, the number of deaths per 100 million miles traveled by car is 0.79, by commuter railroad 0.02, and by transit bus 0.01.

LOWER CRIME RISK

According to the American Public Transportation Association, there were 2,072 total property crimes (theft, larceny) reported on buses and commuter rail lines in the year 2001 (the most recent statistics available). By contrast, the FBI's Uniform Crime Report indicates the number of motor vehicles stolen in the U.S. in the year 2002 was 1.2 million. And the number of cars broken into exceeded 2 million in the year 2004.

Also according to the American Public Transportation Association, in 2001 there were 138 violent crimes against patrons reported on commuter rail lines in the U.S., and 1,364 violent crimes against patrons reported on transit buses nationwide. By comparison, the U.S. Department of Justice reports there are about 34,000 carjackings every year. Seventy-four percent of carjackings involve a weapon, and 24 percent result in injuries. According to the FBI, there were 11,000 robberies at gas stations in 2002; firearms were involved in 42 percent of robbery incidents.

GOOGLE LAUNCHES TRANSIT TRIP PLANNER

As this book goes to press, Google is beta-testing a new service called Google Transit. It works like Mapquest; you simply type in the address you want to go to, and Google will show you the best route to get there via public transit. According to Google's website, "At the moment we're only offering this service for the Portland, Oregon, metro area, but we plan to expand to cities throughout the United States and around the world." For more information, go to www.google .com/transit.

In general, criminals avoid public transit systems because they're monitored by closed-circuit video cameras and patrolled by uniformed and nonuniformed security officers. Most public transit systems now have silent alarms as well. These modern safety systems allow the driver to immediately notify police when disruptive behavior occurs. When the silent alarm is triggered, the destination sign on the outside of the bus or train flashes "EMERGENCY—CALL POLICE."

Ironically, the most common crime reported in public transportation systems does not take place on buses, trains, or in subways. It happens in the parking lot. I'm talking about car theft and break-ins to unattended vehicles parked in commuter lots. Aren't you glad you won't have to worry about that?

Transit Tips

A little experience goes a long way when riding public transportation. After a few trips you'll start to feel confident in your ability to navigate the system and get where you need to go. Soon you'll settle into a comfortable routine. But if you've never taken the bus or train before, here are a few beginner's tips.

- Double-check the destination before boarding. This information is displayed prominently on the boarding side of every bus or train.
- Have exact change ready.
- Let exiting passengers off before you board. Allow people with disabilities or special needs to board first.
- Buy a round-trip fare card to avoid waiting in line at fare card machines on your return trip. This is especially important after large events like concerts and ball games.
- If you carry a bag or purse, place the strap around your leg or arm to prevent accidentally leaving it on board.
- Keep all bags and luggage out of the aisles so other passengers don't trip.
- Remember that schedules vary on weekends and holidays. And if you'll be out late, check what time the last trip runs, so you don't miss it.

Following these simple rules will make your public transportation experience more pleasant for you and for other passengers.

Bicycles and Mass Transit: A Winning Combination

One of the best ways to reach virtually all parts of your city without ever setting foot inside a car is to combine bicycling with mass transit. Most public transportation systems around the country now provide convenient bicycle racks on buses or allow bicycles inside commuter rail cars. Here are some tips for taking your bike for a ride.

BIKE TIPS FOR THE BUS

- Load your bike as quickly as possible so you don't delay the bus and elicit snide remarks from other passengers.
- Be sure your bike is stowed properly in the exterior rack.
- Make sure the driver sees you while you're loading and unloading your bike. Make eye contact.
- When your bike is on an exterior rack, try to sit toward the front of the bus so you can keep your bike in view.
- When exiting the bus, alert the driver that you will be unloading your bicycle.
- Never step to the street side of the bus to load or unload your bike.

CAR-FREE IN PROVO, UTAH

You really have to say "how can I adapt my lifestyle to take advantage of the available transit?" rather than "how can transit best serve the lifestyle that I have already chosen?" One other important thing to mention about the convenience of transit is that you can get things done when you are on the bus or train. I have read a *ton* of books during the past few years that I would never have read if I hadn't had my daily transit time. I have also been able to work on my laptop computer. In fact, I started typing up my answers to these questions when I got on the bus this morning, and now I'm almost to where I get off the bus.

—Travis Jensen, 29, engineer

BIKE TIPS FOR THE TRAIN

- If you take your bike on a commuter rail car, hold the bike at all times and do not use the kickstand.
- Squeeze the bike's brake handle when the train is accelerating or coming to a stop to prevent the bike from rolling.
- Don't force your way onto a crowded train with your bike; wait for the next one.
- Keep your bike out of the aisles and away from the doors.
- Never ride your bike on the train platform; always walk it.
- If your bike is muddy or wet, spray it clean and wipe it down before boarding.

Getting the Best Deal

Most public transit agencies offer several different fare rates. The highest rate is usually the single trip fare. To ride Metrolink buses or commuter rail in St. Louis, for example, costs $1.50 for adults, and seventy-five cents for children and seniors. A monthly pass for unlimited use is $55 for adults and $25 for children and seniors. In many cities you can also buy weekly passes, student passes, semester passes, and college universal passes.

Some employers also have a negotiated rate with mass transit providers. Your employer may even be able to automatically deduct a certain amount from your paycheck, pretax, to use toward

CAR-LITE IN PORTLAND, OREGON

Most mass transit systems these days have good websites. Just like Mapquest, you can type in your start and end addresses, and it'll tell you the route to take, which trains or buses to take and when. If you have a train system nearby, get a map and study it a bit. If there are just buses, then figure out what are the buses that run near you, or between you and work or you and downtown. Try riding them sometime when you're not in a hurry; sit near the driver and ask them where to get off. I've never felt like I was in danger on a train or a bus. On the train, I often see people using laptop computers, messing with cell phones, and using iPods, so clearly these folks aren't worried about getting robbed.

—Isaac Jones, 26, senior software engineer

commuting expense. To learn more about this program visit www
.commutercheck.com. To make sure you're getting the best deal, be
sure to visit your local transit provider's website, or call to request a
new rider information kit.

Try It, You'll Like It

The best way to make up your mind about public transit is to give
it a try. Plan a test trip for a Saturday or Sunday afternoon and
make a few mental notes of what you like and don't like about your
experience. Your goal is to get a sense of whether public transit
would work for your daily commute.

Be aware going in that this will feel different from your old
routine of commuting by car. So view it as an adventure. Experiment. Enjoy the ride. And always remember how much money
you'll be saving.

TRANSIT TIPS

The first time I go somewhere new on a bus, I usually explain that it is my first
time on this line and ask the driver if he will call out my stop. They are usually
happy to do so. If you are confused about fare costs or when the bus comes or
when to pay, ask someone who is standing at your stop. They most likely have
ridden before and can help you. Here are some etiquette tips:

- If you talk on your cell phone, do so quietly. Other people don't want to
  hear your conversation.
- If you and another passenger are engaged in conversation, sit together, not
  across the aisle from each other.
- Don't put a wet umbrella on the seat next to you. Someone will sit there
  later.
- If you are commuting during rush hour and the train is crowded, don't put
  your backpack on the seat next to you. You are making someone who wants
  to sit down have to ask if they can have the seat.

—Patricia Collins, 30, never owned a car

CHAPTER II

Carpooling and Ridesharing

*"You must be the change you
wish to see in the world."*

—Mahatma Gandhi

If three business professionals live in the same suburban neighborhood and work in the same downtown office tower, the American way is for each of them to drive their own car to work. So instead of combining their trips, they'll pay three times as much for parking, burn three times as much gas, emit three times the pollution, take up three times the space on the highway, and spend three times more money than they need to.

Sadly, this is a habit for the vast majority of commuters in this country. According to the 2000 U.S. Census, of the 112 million Americans who drive to work, 87 percent drive alone. That's more than 97 million cars and trucks with just a single person inside.

There is a better, more efficient way that does not involve public transportation.

The Benefits of Carpooling

With gas prices on the rise, carpooling is undergoing a surge in popularity. Nearly fifteen million Americans commute regularly by carpool, according to the 2000 U.S. Census.

Carpooling conserves gas, relieves stress, saves time, cuts parking costs, reduces air pollution, diminishes traffic jams, and saves money. Another huge benefit of carpooling—for both driver and passenger—is that vehicles with more than one person on board can use high-occupancy vehicle (HOV) lanes. This allows carpoolers to zip by solo drivers who are stuck in traffic. Using HOV lanes can cut a commute time in half in many cities.

Carpooling on the Superhighway

In the past few years, carpooling has joined the information superhighway. Just as eBay created an efficient marketplace by linking buyers and sellers through a sophisticated website, so too has the Internet helped people interested in carpooling. Websites like www.erideshare.com, www.carpoolconnect.com, www.carpoolworld.com, and www.craigslist.org in the United States, and www.carpooltool.com in Canada have created online matching services for would-be carpoolers.

All you have to do is register at the website, then view the listings. Each listing states the city or town where the ride originates, the destination, days per week (such as "MTWTF"), and contact information for the person trying to organize the car-

> "People are realizing that they can save thousands of dollars a year by carpooling. At the same time, they know that they're helping to reduce our dependence on foreign oil and reducing greenhouse gas emissions by sharing the ride."
>
> —STEVEN SCHOEFFLER, EXECUTIVE DIRECTOR OF ERIDESHARE.COM

CAR-LITE IN SANTA BARBARA, CALIFORNIA

The carpool that I started is among a group of friends. What we do is contact each other when we have a need to go to a particular store, like the farmers' market, feed store, Trader Joe's (supermarket), or garden supply store, and then several of us pile in a car and do our individual shopping. This has been a really fun way to get together with friends. We often talk about things that are going on around town and just generally catch up. Also the huge benefit now has been that we save money in gas and have several fewer cars on the road at peak shopping times! I suggest that people talk to their friends and find out where, when, and how often they go to the same stores. Start slow, and see how easy it gets from there.

—Eileen Daly, 42, accounts manager

pool. There is also a place for additional notes, such as the time each ride leaves in the morning.

eRideShare.com also has a section for long-distance carpools for out-of-town travel, and carpools specifically for running local errands. By the way, a car is not required; people without cars are invited to join and participate by sharing expenses.

Safety

Most carpooling websites use anonymous email messaging to protect members' identities until there is a match. So when you correspond electronically with a prospective carpooler, that person does not know your name, address, or phone number.

Once you think you have a match, eRideShare.com recommends meeting in a public place before agreeing to carpool together. This is a good time to discuss specifics like eating and drinking in the car, as well as driving safety.

If you decide to carpool with this person, take a few precautions first. Photocopy and exchange copies of your driver's licenses and a list of emergency contacts, as well as personal and employment references. Verifying where a person works and how long he's worked there and calling references are good ways to put your mind at ease. Also, copy down the car license plate number, make, and model. I even suggest photographing the driver and his car, just to be safe. Then make copies of all this information, including the photographs, and give it to a friend or coworker.

This may sound like a lot of precautions, but one can never be too careful. If you're still unsure about your potential carpool partner, agree to a one-month trial period. Chances are your trepidation about riding with a stranger will be unfounded, and your carpool buddy will probably become a good friend.

Finding a Carpool the Old-Fashioned Way

If you're not comfortable hooking up with a stranger through a carpooling website, you can look for a carpool the traditional way. Hanging up a flyer at work or at school is a good start. Ask around at the office or on campus to see if anyone lives in your part of town. Ask people in your neighborhood if they know anyone who works near you. You could even post a "carpool wanted" sign in front of your house or in your apartment complex.

Carpooling Tips

Here are a few carpooling tips from the Wisconsin Department of Transportation's excellent website:

- Establish guidelines up front, so everyone in the carpool knows the expectations.
- Make sure the driver has proper auto insurance and that he notifies his insurance company that he is participating in a carpool.
- Decide when, how, and how often expenses will be paid to the driver.
- When splitting expenses, be sure to include parking costs.
- Be on time. Waiting for passengers who aren't ready frustrates other carpool members and may even get you booted from the group.
- If you know you're going to be late, call ahead and let the driver know.
- Agree on policies regarding eating in the car, smoking, radio stations, and so on.
- All parties should try to remain flexible to accommodate delays and minor emergencies.
- Establish backup plans for when the car breaks down or the driver is sick or takes a vacation.
- Maintain excellent hygiene and grooming habits.
- Avoid wearing cologne or perfume.
- Remember that some people prefer quiet time, especially in the morning.
- Avoid controversial topics of conversation.
- If you decide to leave the carpool, give your carpool partners a few weeks' notice to make other arrangements. Ask them for the same courtesy.

Local Ridesharing and Vanpooling Organizations

Many large metropolitan areas have their own local carpool or rideshare organizations. Call your local Park and Ride office or your local public transit system to inquire. Or do a Google search by typing "[your city]"+"rideshare" or "[your city]"+"ridefinder" or "[your city]"+"carpool." Almost all carpool matching services are provided free of charge. Some cities have even started providing incentives to carpoolers, like gift certificates and prize drawings.

If you have five or more people going to the same place, you may qualify for a vanpool. This is a program in which a local transit system provides a passenger van along a specified route in exchange for a reasonable monthly fare—usually between $70 and $160 per month per person. Vanpools are typically more structured than informal carpools. And vanpools work best with longer commutes, like twenty or thirty miles.

Unlike taking the bus, the route and schedule are determined by the vanpool members. One of the vanpool members drives the van, and other vanpool members volunteer as backup drivers. Vanpooling is often organized with employer or government support. The city of Los Angeles is so desperate to get cars off highways it has been known to offer $1,800 incentives for new vanpools.

Slugging

Slugging is a form of informal carpooling that began in the Washington, D.C., area, where the first HOV lanes were built in the 1970s. It has since spread to other large urban centers like Houston and the San Francisco Bay Area.

Slugging relies on a loosely organized system of pick-up and drop-off points where single drivers can invite total strangers into their car for a ride. With added passengers, the car qualifies to drive in the HOV lane, dramatically reducing commute times. Drivers looking for passengers hold up a sign that signals their destination, then sluggers who are going to the same area hop in. No money is exchanged.

There are now several websites, a newsletter, at least one book, and a published list of etiquette rules for slugging. It's grown into a small industry. For more information on slugging, visit www.slug-lines.com (which focuses on slugging in the Washington, D.C., and Virginia area).

Be Patient

If you've never done it, you may be a little wary of this whole carpool thing. Well, don't give up before you give it a try. Remember, nearly fifteen million people in this country carpool to work every day.

Also keep in mind that it may take a couple of weeks before your carpool settles into a reliable routine. Be patient. Eventually it will become a smoothly operating machine that gets you to work on time, at a fraction of the cost of driving yourself.

CHAPTER 12

Motorcycles and Scooters

*"Owning a car is expensive and pointless
when it's only one person and a briefcase."*

—MATTHEW PATTON, MOTORCYCLE COMMUTER

When researching this book, I put out a request for motorcycle commuters to participate in an interview about biking to work. Within three days I had received so many email messages, they filled my inbox and clogged my email system for about a week. That tells me there are an awful lot of people out there who are passionate about riding motorcycles as daily transportation. As you read some of the success stories in this chapter you'll begin to understand why.

Motorcyclists Are a Growing Group

Motorcycle sales have increased every year for the past twelve years in a row. Back in 1993 the total number of new motorcycles sold in the United States was 293,000. Ten years later, in 2003, motorcycle sales topped one million.

The president of the Motorcycle Industry Council, Tim Buche, says, "Our industry's twelve-year growth cycle is nothing short of spectacular. Motorcycling today is more mainstream than ever—and the numbers prove it." Buche added, "A wider range of Americans are becoming motorcyclists."

*"It is said that you will
find no motorcycles
parked in front of
the therapist's office.
That is, unless it is the
therapist's motorcycle."*

—UNKNOWN

According to the Motorcycle Industry Council:

- The number of female motorcycle owners increased from 6.4 percent in 1990 to 9.6 percent in 2003.
- The median age of motorcycle riders is forty-two.
- Twenty-nine percent of motorcycle riders have college degrees.
- The median household income of motorcycle riders is higher than the median for the U.S. population as a whole.

The surge in popularity is partly due to a better product and wider selection. Today you'll find a larger variety of styles and designs to choose from than ever before. There is a bike made for virtually every skill level and usage pattern. And thanks to computer-aided engineering and advances in metal and plastics technologies, motorcycles are better than ever. Reliability and power have increased, and so has fuel efficiency. Tremendous strides have also been made in safety features and safety equipment.

U.S. MOTORCYCLE SALES	
YEAR	TOTAL
1992	278,000
1993	293,000
1994	306,000
1995	309,000
1996	330,000
1997	356,000
1998	432,000
1999	546,000
2000	710,000
2001	850,000
2002	936,000
2003	1,001,000

Source: Motorcycle Industry Council

The Benefits of Commuting on Two Wheels

Motorcycles and scooters consume less fuel than cars. They take up a smaller amount of space on the highway than cars, so they help reduce traffic congestion. And three to five motorcycles or scooters can park in a spot designed for a single car.

"The twentieth century has heard the call of the motorcycle and answered it. Even the automobile has been forced to admit that it has a real peer in its agile little contemporary."

—EXCERPT FROM "YOU AND THE MOTORCYCLE," EXCELSIOR-HENDERSON, CIRCA 1914

Plus, the cost to purchase, own, and operate a motorcycle or scooter is a fraction of what a car costs. You'll save money on gasoline, tires, insurance, and maintenance, just to name a few. And motorcycle or scooter parking is often free.

Another huge benefit is that most states allow motorcycles free access to HOV lanes. This alone can shave a hefty chunk of time off of a commute. It's one of many reasons motorcycles can be a faster way to travel through a city. A British study found that riding a motorcycle or scooter in London reduced travel time by 40 to 60 percent. Maybe that's why scooter sales in the U.K. have risen 1,600 percent, from five hundred in 1993 to eight thousand in 2004, according to the Motorcycle Industry Association.

And let's not forget that riding a motorcycle is fun, it's a great conversation starter, and motorcyclists just seem cool. How great would it be to start and end your workday doing something you truly enjoy?

CAR-LITE IN SANTA CLARITA, CALIFORNIA

I bought my motorcycle for $900. I paid for it in full, so there is no monthly payment.

Registration: $100 per year.

Insurance: $170 per year (basic liability only).

Gas: approximately $20 per week (assuming $2.60 per gallon) = $1,040 per year. (My motorcycle commute is fifty miles round trip—twenty-five miles in each direction. This amounts to 12,000 miles per year.)

Parking: $0—even when I go out to lunch in a mall where I used to pay for parking, the attendant allows me to park for free as long as I don't take up a parking space. I park alongside a curb or a tree.

Maintenance: $90 per year in oil changes (every 4,000 miles); $400 per year in tires (assuming a change every 5,000 to 7,000 miles); $90 per year in brake pads.

Total annual motorcycle costs: $1,890.

The car we sold was a Honda Civic Hybrid, so it got about the same gas mileage. Our monthly car payment was $380. Registration was about $300 per year. Insurance was about $1,200 per year.

Total annual car costs: Approximately $7,700 per year. The motorcycle saves us approximately $5,810 per year.

—Tony Guinta, 36, IT project manager

Lane Sharing

Another way motorcyclists get to work faster than people driving cars is by a method variously called filtering, lane sharing, or lane splitting. Where allowed, it means motorcyclists may ride between lanes of traffic gridlock on a multilane highway. Lane sharing is legal in some states, including California.

Some motorcyclists think lane sharing is dangerous; others say it is one of the safest ways to ride. This debate will certainly continue, but for now just know that lane sharing is definitely not a tactic for beginning riders. There are safe lane-sharing methods and unsafe ones, so it may be something to look into once you have a few years of experience, and only if it's legal in your state.

Motorcycle Safety Concerns

Motorcycles have a reputation for being dangerous. And statistically, they are more dangerous than cars. According to a 1999 study by the National Highway Transportation Safety Administration, per vehicle mile motorcyclists are sixteen times more likely to die in a crash than people who drive cars.

But to get the full story we have to look deeper into the numbers. According to the NHTSA:

- Forty-one percent of motorcyclists who died in fatal crashes were speeding at the time of the crash (versus 31 percent for all motor vehicle fatalities).

CAR-LITE IN COLUMBIA, ILLINOIS

When you join the ranks of two-wheeled commuters, you are joining a worldwide family. Most motorcyclists wave when they approach another motorcyclist on the road. The wave is an acknowledgment that we are a different breed from the "cagers" (automobile drivers). The wave is a tip o' the hat to the fact that we, as motorcyclists, face an entirely different set of challenges out on the road compared to the average commuter. Whatever wave you use, make sure you exercise your right to celebrate your membership in an exclusive group.

—John Anderson, 42, television cameraman

- Almost half of the motorcycle operators who died in single-vehicle crashes were intoxicated (versus 30 percent for all motor vehicle fatalities).
- Almost one-third of motorcyclists who died in crashes did not have a proper license.
- Almost half of motorcyclists who died in crashes were not wearing a helmet.
- Seventy percent of all crashes occurred on undivided roadways.
- The average motorcycle is ridden only about 1,800 total miles per year (versus 14,600 miles for the average car).

The lessons from this study are clear: follow common sense, and get proper motorcycle training *before* you ride. If you maintain a safe speed, obtain the proper motorcycle license, wear a helmet, don't drink and ride, and ride regularly you can drastically reduce your likelihood of being injured on a motorcycle. And since most fatalities happen on undivided roadways, keep in mind that you are actually safer commuting to work on an interstate or other divided highway. Experts say daily riding experience is invaluable and that the risk per mile goes down the more often one rides.

SHOULD YOU WEAR A HELMET?

Regardless of the law, which varies from state to state, common sense and safety require that all motorcycle and scooter riders wear a helmet. This goes for every trip on the bike, regardless of

CAR-LITE IN CALGARY, ALBERTA

The first time I rode my motorcycle to my new job, I got ready to go home by changing into my riding gear in the office washroom. I walked out in leather chaps, riding boots, motorcycle jacket, and fingerless gloves. I found myself face-to-face with the senior partner of the company. He just blinked at me for a few seconds and then said, "You ride a motorcycle?" I was thinking that maybe at this company it was not appropriate for the senior customer service manager to be a biker, but I said "Yes" anyway. A look of relief came over his face. He exhaled and said, "Thank God. I thought you might be one of the Village People."

—Don Morberg, 56, customer service manager

distance. Experienced riders point out that cyclists should also always wear protective clothing such as leather jackets, chaps, or armored riding suits. Avoid riding in flimsy clothing like shorts, T-shirts, and sandals.

TAKE A MOTORCYCLE COURSE FIRST

If you think commuting by motorcycle might be for you, the first step is to become a properly licensed rider and take a motorcycle rider's safety course. Many community colleges and vocational schools offer comprehensive courses that cover everything from buying a bike to rules of the road and safety procedures. You don't even need your own motorcycle to take the course; the instructor or the school will make at least one demonstration model available to students.

A national organization called the Motorcycle Safety Foundation sponsors courses around the country. They have an informative website (www.msf-usa.org) and a toll-free number (800-446-9227) to call for course information and locations in your area. The automated phone response system works very efficiently: just enter your zip code and you'll get a listing of course locations in your area.

The MSF also has a number of booklets that you can download for free from their website, including an eighty-six-pager, *You and Your Motorcycle: Riding Tips,* and a forty-four-pager, the *Motorcycle Operator's Manual.* You may want to download and read these booklets before signing up for a course.

CAR-FREE IN SAN FRANCISCO, CALIFORNIA

Parking is a bear in San Francisco, thus I haven't owned a car since 1984. I hire a cage when I need to, which is more infrequent than I imagined. The cost of renting a car is far below the cost of owning a car (car payments, insurance and parking tickets) and I get a brand new car every time. My motorbike is the perfect vehicle for metropolitan living: fuel efficient, traffic efficient, easy to park, and just plain fun to ride.

—Michael J. "Dr. Geese" Graphix, 48, production manager

Why Not Ride a Two-Wheeler to Work?

Below is a list of objections commonly raised against using a motorcycle as daily transportation, and a response to each. This list is from the website of a motorcycle accessories company called Aerostich Riderwear. Their website (www.aerostich.com) has many excellent products, resources, and how-to articles for daily riding. The list is reprinted verbatim below with permission from the company and from the author, Andy Goldfine.

**TOP ELEVEN REASONS NOT TO RIDE
A MOTORCYCLE TO WORK ADDRESSED**

- **How can I learn this?** Riding to work and for transportation is not as simple as using a car or public transit. Seek experienced commuting or transportation riders for lessons, information, and mentoring. You'll find commute-savvy riders by networking at local motorcycle groups, shops, and clubs.
- **Takes too much extra time.** Studies show that net motorcycle commuting times are the same as, or slightly faster than commuting by car. So even with the extra steps of dressing in riding gear, you'll be ahead. To prove it, motorcycle every day for two weeks. The first week will be practice to establish riding routines. Time each trip during the second week and average them. Then drive for a week and average those times. Compare the two averages.
- **There is no safe place to leave my bike at work.** This is common. Work with your employer or with a nearby property owner to arrange a suitable place. Ideally, it should be secure from theft and

CAR-LITE IN CHICAGO, ILLINOIS

Commuting by motorcycle is a fast and efficient means of private transportation. Scooters are even more efficient in high-density urban environments. Unfortunately, in this country motorcycles are typically seen as luxury items or lifestyle accessories rather than as a legitimate means of transportation. If motorcycles were more mainstream, as they are in Europe, we would all have less urban traffic gridlock and commuters would shave significant amounts of time from their daily commute.

—Anthony Tam, 30, web application QA tester

tampering, shaded, and convenient to your work area. Offer (or be willing) to pay for a good place. Leave a cover or lock permanently stationed at your spot. A locker or plastic bin can be secured to a fence or wall to contain both items, or store other gear.

- **Errands.** Kids, groceries, shopping . . . you can use packs, courier bags, saddlebags, tank bags, bungees, and racks to carry a surprising amount. Most school age children can be readily transported by bike, but you'll need to carry their gear (helmet/jacket/gloves) for them. Children of all ages are routine bike and scooter passengers in many countries outside of the U.S. If you've been buying a month of groceries with your car, change to buying a week's worth on your bike.

- **Work clothing is not suitable.** Keep a sport coat, suit, uniform, or changes of work-suitable clothing at work. Or pack a change of work clothing along in a courier bag or duffel. Or wear a coverall-type riding suit.

- **Employer says no.** Explain how riding energizes and leaves one more alert. Regular motorcycle commuting improves concentration, risk management skills, and overall health. Provide documentation from motorcycling advocacy sources like *The Daily Rider* (www.ridetowork.org) about the broader societal values, too. Use creative methods like sending a plant with an environmental pro-riding note. Follow a few weeks later with a box of candies and another note about parking advantages. A fruit basket with a third note about health benefits a month later. And so on.

- **Commute distance is too long or short.** Get a more comfortable motorcycle. Lots of people do daily 100+ mile commutes on touring bikes. Lots of people do one-mile commutes on small scooters.

CAR-FREE IN HIAWASSEE, GEORGIA

I am a lawyer, and an investor, and ride my Harley-Davidson Electra Glide everywhere I go. I do not own a car, and have absolutely no desire to acquire one. Riding a bike as your only transportation, especially a Harley, always brings out conversations with total strangers that would never arise if I were arriving in a car. I am fifty-six years old and started riding in 1992. I have used a bike as my sole transportation since 1996. Most people probably consider me to be somewhat of a rebel, or a renegade, and they are right on the money!

—Frank Boorn, 56, attorney

- **No cell phone audio and coffee.** Weatherproof radios, helmet speakers, or ear speaker systems are all available, as are various functional cup holders and hands-fee phone brackets. Look for these (and more) in motorcycle magazine advertisements, and from accessory catalogs or at shops.
- **Riding is too dirty.** Wash your face and hands upon arriving at work. Wear protective clothing when riding. Change clothing as needed.
- **Traffic is dangerous.** Damn straight it is. But if you can drive to work for years without an accident, you can learn to do it just as safely on a motorcycle. Ride paranoid and keep your riding skills sharp and you should never have a problem. Without an automobile capsule, you'll need to be visible and wear protective gear.
- **It's too much work.** And sometimes it rains. Get over it. And get a rain suit.

FURTHER READING

- *Street Strategies: A Survival Guide for Motorcyclists,* by David Hough
- *Proficient Motorcycling: The Ultimate Guide to Riding Well,* by David Hough
- *The Complete Idiot's Guide to Motorcycles,* by Darwin Holmstrom
- *Ride Hard, Ride Smart: Ultimate Street Strategies for Advanced Motorcyclists,* by Pat Hahn

Scoot to Commute

Scooters differ from motorcycles in several ways. They have smaller engines, usually between 50 and 250 cc's. They don't go quite as fast as motorcycles, but they get better gas mileage. Scooters have automatic transmissions, so there's no clutch to worry about.

Scooters usually have a "step-through" design so you can put your legs directly in front of you while riding. And scooters weigh less than motorcycles, so they're easier to handle. For example, pulling a scooter up over a six-inch curb is doable; good luck trying that with a seven-hundred-pound motorcycle. It is a good idea to secure a lightweight scooter with a chain and lock.

CAR-LITE IN SAN JOSE, CALIFORNIA

I commute to work every day on a Vespa scooter. I save about two grand a year just on gas. Unless I'm traveling with someone other than my girlfriend or transporting things that are too awkward or large for my scooter there is no reason to use a car.

—Josh Rogers, 31, advertising director

CONVENIENT AROUND TOWN

If you live within ten miles of work, a small 50cc scooter may be an ideal form of daily transportation. With a top speed of around forty miles per hour, it will get you everywhere you need to go as long as you stay off major highways. You can add saddlebags or racks to carry groceries, and you can park it just about anywhere. If your commute requires highway travel, you'll need a larger scooter. Some 250cc models can reach eighty-five miles per hour and easily keep up with interstate highway traffic. Check your local highway regulations to see if there are restrictions or limitations regarding scooters on the interstate.

According to Stephen Zompa, owner of Vespa St. Louis (www .vespastl.com), "The big benefit of the newer scooters is the fact that storage compartments are plentiful. And with top cases and side cases totaling six cubic feet of storage, you could easily fit your full grocery list. And 100 miles per gallon isn't bad either."

CAR-LITE IN ST. LOUIS, MISSOURI

I use my Vespa ET2 scooter every day and have put over 1,000 miles on it in the last three and a half months. I usually have to put gas in every ten days or so, but the tank only holds two and a half gallons. I don't run it dry and I never spend more than four dollars to fill it. Scooters are very Euro-chic and garner a lot of attention. Mine is red. I am not only visible, I am practically a traffic hazard because I cause rubber-necking.

—Loren Jenks, broker

AFFORDABLE TRANSPORTATION

You can buy a new Honda scooter starting at about $1,800. A new Italian-made Vespa will set you back around $3,000 for the entry-level model. Off-brand scooters made in China are available for under $1,000. The cost to insure a scooter can be as low as $150 per year. Some models get more than one hundred miles per gallon. And there is usually no cost to park a scooter.

Since scooters cost less than motorcycles and get better gas mileage, they're selling so fast many dealers can't keep them in stock. In 1997 the total number of scooters sold in the U.S. was around twelve thousand. By 2003 that number jumped to eighty-four thousand. And in 2004 sales topped one hundred thousand.

Laws regarding scooters vary. In many states, scooters with 50cc engines are considered mopeds. Thus they do not require any special licensing. But it's important to keep in mind that any motorized vehicle can be dangerous and requires proper training to operate. All scooter buyers should sign up for a motorcycle training course, wear a helmet at all times, and obey the traffic laws. Check with your local Honda or Vespa dealer for more information.

CAR-LITE IN ST. LOUIS, MISSOURI

Most people think of motor scooters as relatively small and somewhat slow. If you are one of them you are in for a surprise. My Piaggio BV200 has a top speed of seventy-five mph. Using the scooter to go to work, run errands, or drive through the park is a wonderful experience. Try it, you will love it.

—John Hungerford, mid-60s, stockbroker

CHAPTER 13

Bicycling

> *"Every time I see an adult on a bicycle,*
> *I no longer despair for the human race."*
>
> —H. G. WELLS

Wouldn't it be great if someone invented a form of personal transportation that:

- Is practically free
- Is immediately available on demand
- Doesn't require any licensing, taxes, stickers, or fees
- Could travel faster than cars stuck in traffic
- Doesn't pollute the environment
- Helps us get exercise while we're using it
- Doesn't make us pay for parking
- Doesn't force us to pay high gas prices
- Helps boost our self-confidence
- Improves our outlook on life

Gosh, that would be great. Now go buy a bicycle.

The Benefits of Bicycle Commuting

The bicycle is the most efficient mode of human transport ever devised. The only form of transportation that's cheaper is walking. And if you factor in that biking saves time by covering more ground more quickly, walking may not even be cheaper. There are so many benefits to commuting by bicycle, we can't possibly list them all in this chapter. So here is the highlight reel of why you should consider commuting with pedal power.

IT SAVES MONEY

When you commute by bicycle you have no monthly car payment, no gas to buy, no parking to pay for, no oil changes, no car washes, no finance charges, no insurance premiums, no license or registration fees, no personal property taxes—and the list goes on. You may spend $200 or so per year on maintenance and equipment for a bike, but even that is offset by other savings. For example, when you get your daily exercise by riding to work, you may decide to cancel your gym membership.

In England, listeners to BBC Radio were asked to vote in an online poll for the most significant invention since the year 1800. The overwhelming winner was the bicycle, with 59 percent of the vote. The transistor came in second with 8 percent.

Plus, the cost of entry into the world of bicycle commuting is low. There's no need to spend $1,000 on a fancy road bike. Not yet, anyway. You can buy a decent used bicycle for around $150. Add another $30 for a safety check and tune-up at your local bike shop, plus $50 for a good (new) helmet and $60 for a sturdy lock. For under $300 you are ready to get out and ride.

Now compare that to the $8,000 the average American spends *every year* to own and operate a car. Trading your car for a bicycle may literally be your ticket to easy street, in more ways than one.

IT WILL MAKE YOU HEALTHIER

If you commute to work in a car every day, you have two choices. You can either sacrifice an additional hour of your free time to fit in a daily workout, or you can just accept being overweight, out of

CAR-LITE IN SAN DIEGO, CALIFORNIA

I've saved thousands upon thousands of dollars because of bicycle commuting. My retirement account is very flush with those savings. I'll be able to do a whole lotta' biking in my retirement!

—Frank Paiano, 48

shape, and unhealthy. According to the American Medical Association, 60 percent of Americans lead completely sedentary lifestyles. And as you know, lack of exercise can lead to heart disease, diabetes, and many other health problems.

Bicycle commuting is a guaranteed way to get moderate physical activity five days a week. Cycling burns about five hundred calories

per hour. It exercises your heart, lungs, and muscles. It tones and firms arms, legs, shoulders, abs, and buttocks. It burns fat and increases metabolism. It helps you lose weight without dieting. It builds your immune system and makes you less likely to get sick. It reduces the risk of heart attack and stroke. And it's considered low-impact exercise, so you won't damage your knees or other joints. It may even help you live longer. Plus, you're exercising *while you're commuting*, which saves time.

So why sit on your butt in a car in rush-hour traffic, clogging your arteries with fast food and watching your waistline expand, when you could be losing weight, getting in shape, and building a healthier body? All this while saving a ton o' cash!

YOU'LL AVOID TRAFFIC JAMS

Even the fastest cars slow to a crawl when they get caught in a traffic jam. Some studies show the average speed of a car in city traffic

CAR-LITE IN CHICAGO, ILLINOIS

I hate to think that some overweight people, elderly, or people with kids think they can't ride a bike or walk for transportation. Once they start doing it, it just gets easier, like yoga or anything else. Then they get the accruing returns of increased energy, better joint health and bone density, less depression, etc.

—Lisa Phillips, project coordinator

is less than fifteen miles per hour. Bicycle commuters, on the other hand, never sit in bumper-to-bumper traffic. If there's an accident, they can ride around it on the sidewalk, bike lane, or wide shoulder. If a road is shut down for construction, they can cut through a city park or take a bike path. With an average speed of ten to twenty miles per hour, an experienced cyclist can make a five-mile commute in fifteen to thirty minutes.

IT HELPS COMMUNITIES AND THE ENVIRONMENT

According to a study by the U.S. Department of Transportation, "Bicycling and walking conserve roadway and residential space; avert the need to build, service, and dispose of autos; and spare users of public space the noise, speed, and intimidation that often characterize motor vehicle use, particularly in urban areas."

Cycling helps the environment by reducing the use of fossil fuels for transportation. Bicycle riding does not contribute to smog, air pollution, global warming, or other environmental damage caused by locating, extracting, transporting, processing, and burning petroleum. Every time a cyclist makes a four-mile round-trip commute on a bicycle instead of driving a car, she prevents fifteen pounds

CAR-FREE IN PORTLAND, OREGON

I finally got up the courage to buy a bicycle and start commuting to school. It was scary at first. I wasn't in shape at all. And I didn't have anyone to get good advice from, so now I see how many mistakes I made (just a small example: no fenders in Portland!). Still, every day it got easier, and every day I liked my trip more and more.

As time went by, I began to feel all kinds of other benefits. I started to feel stronger, and proud of my strong body. I started to really know the city I lived in and be able to get to all kinds of places on my own. I noticed that I was in a better mood all the time, and I was sleeping better. I felt independent and able to take charge of when and how I got somewhere. And I use the money I would have spent on a car to take a big trip every year. In the last few years alone I've been to India, Switzerland, Italy, Spain, France, and South Africa.

—Jessica Roberts, 30, membership director

of toxic tailpipe emissions from polluting the air. When a bicycle replaces a car for daily transportation, we all breathe less carbon monoxide, lead, cyanide, benzene, sulfates, ozone, particulate matter, and volatile organic compounds.

IT'S FUN AND EMPOWERING

The majority of bicycles sold in this country are used for recreation. That's because riding a bike is inherently fun. You feel the sun on your face and the breeze on your skin, and you can smell the trees and flowers. You can greet fellow cyclists and pedestrians verbally as you pass by or wait at a red light. Try doing that in a car.

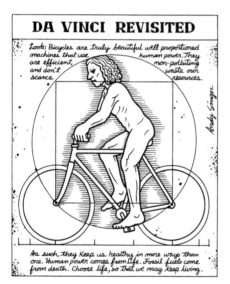

DA VINCI REVISITED

Look: Bicycles are truly beautiful, well proportioned machines that use human power. They are efficient, and don't waste our resources.

As such, they keep us healthy in more ways than one. Human power comes from life. Fossil fuels come from death. Choose life, so that we may keep living.

Bicycle commuting is a great way to start the day invigorated. You'll arrive at work refreshed, alert, and full of energy and endorphins. It's also an effective way to relax *after* work, guaranteed time to exercise away the day's stress. You may even find yourself extending your ride to maximize your time in the seat.

Commuting under your own power will boost your self-esteem and self-confidence. Many bike commuters report a feeling of accomplishment, empower-

CAR-LITE IN COLLIER COUNTY, FLORIDA

I'm fifty-eight years old and I use a mountain bike for commuting and there's absolutely nothing that can stop me from getting to work. I love to be outside, and there's no downside to this. It's great just ignoring the worst traffic jams.

—Stan Chrzanowski, engineering review manager

ment, and self-reliance. In contrast, car commuters often complain of feeling powerless sitting in traffic and helpless at the gas pump as prices rise.

Choosing a Bike

Do not go out and buy a brand-new $1,000 bike rigged out with the best commuting gear money can buy. Don't even buy a $500 bike. Because at this point, you don't know what type of bike you need, or even if bicycle commuting is something you'll enjoy.

JOIN AN AMAZING URBAN ADVENTURE RACE

For the past several months, I have been enrolled in the most amazing Eco Challenge–style urban adventure race. There is no entry fee, no competition, and no finish line, though there are some applauding folks along the way. And the prizes exceed imagination.

After numerous "pre-race briefings'" and practice runs I was ready. I sold my car and went full-time car-free and carefree (with a little help from friends and mass transit). The long, rugged course lay before me. Day after day, my challenge was to arrive at my job, pick up groceries, and visit friends and relatives, all without a car.

Most of the segments of this race are on a bicycle. Bonuses are awarded for hitting green space, avoiding traffic and pollution, and using pedestrian overpasses, walkways, and other links that are inaccessible to cars.

Urban adventure racers might seem like they are having more fun than can possibly be legal within the allotted twenty-four hours each day. By avoiding senseless errands and purchases, traffic lights and traffic jams, gas stations, trips to the gym, half-hour drives to get a fifteen-minute dose of "nature," car trips where you feel trapped, sullied, or "owned" by your car, they are actually saving time and money, improving health, and enjoying every minute of it!

The day I sold my car, it felt like a two-ton weight (plus or minus a tire jack) had been lifted off my shoulders. The past few months have been among the happiest of my life. I feel peace every day in that no matter how much or how little I accomplish, I have already accomplished this: I have cared for others, made the world a little better place to live, and perhaps best of all, inspired someone else to do the same.

—Rudy Schwarz, urban bicyclist

If you already own a bicycle, use it—provided it's safe, functional, and relatively suited to the purpose. If you don't have a bike, borrow one. If you can't borrow one, buy a used bike for a fraction of the cost of a new one.

If you decide later that bicycle commuting is something you definitely want to do, then go spend as much money as you want. However, the advantage of buying a quality used bike is that if it gets stolen you're not out all that much money. I still commute on the same secondhand bike I paid $150 for nearly three years ago.

Whatever bike you use for this trial period, be sure to have an experienced bike mechanic perform a complete safety check before you ride it in traffic. Also, make sure the bike is adjusted to your height and body size. While you're at the local bike shop, buy a quality (brand-new) bicycle helmet, and ask the staff to help you adjust it properly.

Choosing Your Route

The next step is finding the *best* route for your bicycle commute. Note that I did not write "finding the *fastest* route." There's a big difference.

When cycling, safety is the number-one concern. If there's a street that runs straight from your home to your office, great. But if that street is poorly lit, is filled with speeding cars, has narrow shoulders and broken pavement, and is covered in gravel, then you want to avoid it.

CAR-FREE IN ATLANTA, GEORGIA

It takes me about the same time to commute by bike as it does my coworkers who drive in from the same area, and I'm getting physical activity. When there is heavy traffic I beat everyone. People always think I look very nice for someone who just got off her bike. They can't believe I bicycled in a suit or in a skirt (which, having traveled to countries where this is normal, I certainly don't think it is amazing). Most people are impressed. They tell me they wish they lived close enough to bike to work.

—Katie Sobush, 27, planning and policy analyst

In every city or town, some streets are more suitable for auto-mobile travel, others more suitable for bicycle travel. Often the two are just a block away from each other. Here are a few of the differentiators.

THINGS TO LOOK FOR

- A designated bike path or wide shoulder
- Smooth, even pavement
- Streetlights
- Scenic views and tree-lined streets
- Lighter traffic pattern
- Sidewalks
- Proximity to services (like a neighborhood coffee shop)

THINGS TO AVOID

- Roads with heavy traffic
- Roads with fast-moving traffic
- Dangerous intersections
- Poorly lighted areas
- Steep hills
- Potholes or broken pavement
- Sand and gravel on the roadway
- Dangerous drain grates or gutters
- Railroad tracks
- Rumble strips and speed bumps
- Loud traffic noise
- Truck routes
- Narrow bridges or tunnels

Ultimately, you should try to come up with three or four different routes that suit you. You may choose one route on a gorgeous summer day, a different route on a rainy day, and yet another route in the winter when it gets dark earlier.

How Far Can You Go?

Comfortable bicycle commuting distances vary widely by individual fitness level, topography, and personal preference. Some dedicated cyclists ride fifteen miles or more each way. But for the average commuter, three miles or less each way would be considered an easy ride. Six miles is a substantial but very doable ride. And ten miles or more might require some physical training. According to the 2002 National Survey of Pedestrians and Bicyclists conducted by the U.S. Department of Transportation, the average length of a bicycle trip is 3.9 miles.

Carrying Cargo

If you ride to work you may need to carry papers, a notebook computer, lunch, a change of clothes, and so on. Or perhaps you have to run a few errands after work, like a trip to the supermarket or video store. The simplest and easiest way to do this is to use a small backpack. Always keep a few folded plastic garbage bags in the bottom of the backpack so you can keep your stuff dry if it begins to rain.

If you become a serious bicycle commuter you can rig your bike with panniers (saddlebags), baskets, and racks for carrying loads

CAR-FREE IN CHICAGO, ILLINOIS

I've been car-free since 1997. Once you figure out a system, the challenges of living car-free are few. Occasionally I need a vehicle for trips to Home Depot or for moving, and I can ask a friend or rent a vehicle for those occasions.

The lifestyle benefits of living car-free are great. I know that if I had a car I would not be in as good of shape. Emotionally, biking is a cure for the blues and for stress. It's also a boost for the ego to zip by cars stuck in rush hour on city streets. I never get road rage.

The financial benefits of living car-free are wonderful. I do not have to pay car payments, insurance, parking, tickets, towing fees, city stickers, or major repairs. I can't imagine how much money I've saved by not owning a car.

—Jennifer McArdle, production manager

off of your body. There are dozens of excellent cycling gear companies that cater to commuters and touring cyclists. You can even buy folding garment bags designed to carry a business suit on your bike without wrinkling.

Storing Your Bike at Work

With a little creativity this problem is easy to solve. If your bike will fit in a corner of your office, you're golden. If not, ask the property manager to install bike hooks in the ceiling or on the wall to hang your bike. If that fails, ask the custodial staff in your building if there's a utility closet, storage room, or workout facility that has extra space. I've found most housekeeping and custodial workers to be very helpful in this regard, since they know the nooks and crannies of the building better than anyone. A smile and a sincere "thank you" are usually all it takes to get their help.

If your office building does not allow bicycles inside at all, write the management company and ask for special permission. Tell them it's your only mode of transportation. If you don't know whether your building allows bikes, don't ask! Just bring it in and assume it's alright. Chances are no one will ever question you. But if you ask first, there's a chance you'll be denied.

If there's no way to store your bike inside your building, look for a covered parking garage where you can lock your bike securely. If there are plenty of parking spots for cars but no bike racks, take action. Write a letter asking that one parking spot be converted to bike parking.

CAR-LITE IN FERGUSON, MISSOURI

I highly recommend using panniers (saddlebags). They make your bike wider and also provide more surface area to put on reflectors/reflective tape. I have noticed drivers give me more room than if I didn't have them on. Plus you can carry extra clothes in case the temperature changes. I also use them to carry stuff for errands or shopping.

—Jeff Jackson, 30, banker

Try to park your bike where there are people around, instead of in an out-of-the-way place. If someone is going to cut through your lock, they're unlikely to do it where others are watching. Many experienced urban riders suggest using both a rigid U-shaped lock *and* a chain or cable lock. Double locking will deter most thieves.

Riding Safely

The most important part of bicycle commuting is safety. There are many excellent resources and books available that teach safe cycling. Here are some of the basics:

- **See and be seen.** Wear bright-colored clothing and reflectors so motorists will spot you. If you wear a backpack, cover it with reflective tape and clip a red strobe light to the back. Wear reflective leg bands around your ankles; motorists will see the up-and-down motion and immediately know you're a cyclist. Use a headlight and taillight at night. And make sure you can see the road and other drivers, especially when you're bundled up in the winter or in the rain. Always look behind you when changing lanes; a rear-view mirror helps with this.

- **Always wear a helmet.** Wearing a helmet reduces your chances of a head injury by 85 percent. Ask your local bike shop to help you size and adjust the helmet properly. Never buy a used helmet.

- **Obey the rules of the road.** Bicycles are considered vehicles and should follow the same traffic laws that apply to cars. That means stopping at red lights and stop signs. Check with your state for other laws that apply to bicyclists.

- **Ride with traffic.** Do not ride against oncoming traffic. There are too many reasons for this to list here.

- **Ride on the right.** All fifty states require slow-moving vehicles, like bicycles, to ride on the right. Motorists expect slower vehicles on the right.

- **Be predictable.** When you follow the same rules as everyone else, your behavior is predictable. When you're on your own game plan or making up rules as you go, motorists get confused. Confusion can lead to accidents.

- **Communicate.** Always signal your lane changes and turns to let other drivers know where you're going. Assume they do not see you until you're certain they do.

- **Beware of parked cars.** Always ride at least three feet from parked cars so you don't get hit by an opening door. This is the most common cause of injuries to cyclists.
- **Ride in a straight line.** Do not swerve in and out of the roadway or between parked cars.
- **Always ride defensively.** Watch for cars that are driving erratically. Try to avoid other drivers' blind spots. Be ready to take evasive maneuvers when needed.
- **Avoid road hazards.** Wide sewer grates, oil slicks, sand, gravel, utility hole covers, and debris in the roadway can cause you to become more intimately acquainted with the pavement than you would like.
- **Do a quick check before every ride.** Make sure your tires are properly inflated. Make sure your brakes are working. And check your chain, gears, and quick-release levers to make sure they're in order.
- **Take a bicycle safety course.** Safe-cycling classes are offered by many cycling organizations, such as Effective Cycling by the League of American Bicyclists. These courses offer practical on-road training, as well as classroom instruction.
- **Carry water and snacks with you.** If you're cycling long distances it's a good idea to replenish your body with something to eat and keep yourself hydrated during the ride.

Keep in mind the following statistics from the website www .bicyclesource.com:

- Half of all bicycle-car collisions happen at intersections.
- Bicycling against the flow of traffic accounts for about 16 percent of collisions.

RIDE ON THE RIGHT (USUALLY)

Ride as far right as *safely* practicable,

- EXCEPT when passing others or turning left;
- EXCEPT to avoid parked cars, moving vehicles, or people;
- EXCEPT to avoid animals, objects, surface debris, or other hazards;
- EXCEPT in a vehicle lane too narrow for a bicycle and another vehicle to pass safely, side by side, within the lane.

—Lauren Cooper, *The Art and Science of Advanced Traffic Bicycling*

- Only 5 percent of collisions involved a cyclist being hit from behind.

One of the best articles I've seen on bicycle safety appears on the website www.bicyclesafe.com. The author is Michael Bluejay, and the article is "How to Not Get Hit by Cars." Please read this before riding in city traffic. Also, the League of American Bicyclists offers a number of safe-riding courses, including one on commuting. Check out their website at www.bikeleague.org.

FURTHER READING

- *Effective Cycling,* by John Forester
- *Urban Bikers' Tricks and Tips,* by Dave Glowacz
- *The Art of Urban Cycling: Lessons from the Street,* by Robert Hurst
- *The League Guide to Safe and Enjoyable Cycling,* by The League of American Bicyclists
- *Anybody's Bike Book,* by Tom Cuthbertson
- *The Lance Armstrong Performance Program: Seven Weeks to the Perfect Ride,* by Lance Armstrong and Chris Carmichael

Dressing for the Weather

How you dress will be determined by how long your commute is and by weather conditions. If you live within three miles of your workplace and you don't have to climb any steep hills you'll probably be fine wearing your work clothes while you ride. Even in the middle of summer, temperatures at 8:00 A.M. are cool enough in most regions that you won't be covered in sweat by the time you arrive at the office. Remember, too, that when you're riding a bike the wind rushing over you quickly evaporates sweat off your skin. This helps you to stay dry and lowers your body temperature.

Before beginning either leg of your daily bicycle commute, use the Internet to check the local weather radar. Visit www.weather .com and set up a custom home page for your zip code.

If you have a longer commute, or if you live in a hot or humid climate, wear shorts and a T-shirt during your ride, then change into work clothes when you get to the office. Be sure to bring dry socks and underwear. We'll cover wardrobe, appearance, and grooming tips in greater detail in chapter 15.

Rain is not a problem for a well-equipped bicycle commuter. I've seen bicycle commuters wear everything from thin ponchos to rubber rain slickers to full Gore-Tex suits. More than likely, a cheap nylon rain suit will work just fine. Front and rear fenders on your bike will also help keep water from spraying up onto you.

Cycling in Winter

Clothing for winter cycling is similar to what you'd wear to go snow skiing or hiking in the cold. Dress in layers so you can easily shed clothing when your body temperature rises. And your body temperature *will* rise, so start the ride a little underdressed.

Make sure your outer layer is windproof. Winter gloves, a neck gaiter, earmuffs, and even a partial face mask may be in order, depending on the temperature. Some bicycle commuters wear ski goggles to protect their eyes from winter winds. Whatever you wear, be sure you have complete visibility and an unobstructed view of the road and the cars around you.

For cyclists, winter precipitation can be tricky, but not impossible to handle. If you have knobby tires you can probably ride in the snow. But when there's ice on the road, it's time to call a cab or take the bus. If you live in a climate that regularly gets severe winter weather, visit www.icebike.org, a website dedicated to bicycling on snow and ice.

TIPS FROM AN EXPERIENCED BICYCLE COMMUTER

- *Bike clothing.* I always ride in bike clothing and change into work clothing at the office. This works better for me than trying to ride slower and not sweat. I ferry in a week's worth of my clothing via panniers or messenger bag, or by using a bicycle trailer. I take it home in my messenger bag or panniers after I wear it, one outfit at a time. I wear the same pants all week and I change underwear, shirt, and socks daily. No problem. Since I have no car, it is not unreasonable for me to spend a couple of hundred dollars a year to upgrade and maintain my extensive bike clothing wardrobe. There is some really good clothing out there for rainy weather and very cold weather.

- *Distance to commute.* I think dedicated riders can ride much farther more easily. I commuted 11.5 miles each way every day for a couple of years. That took about forty minutes on a good day, fifty minutes when the weather was severe. My commute now is 6.5 hilly miles one way, and I routinely do it in twenty-three minutes or less. I'm fifty-two and not a very fast rider. No big deal. But then, I do sweat a lot.

- *Bike parking.* For about a year I couldn't bring my bike inside at one location. So I found a plastic bike cover in some mail-order catalog that worked great. It was like a big envelope with snaps that secured it at the bottom so it wouldn't blow away in a breeze. However, a waterproof tarp and bungee cords can also serve well in this capacity. I kept it at my office and covered the bike with it during any inclement weather.

- *Drying wet clothing.* I keep a small fan at my office. If my clothing is soaked from rain or sweat or both, I wring it out, hang it, and put the fan close to the wet clothing. I rotate the clothes a couple of times during the day to blow air over them from different angles. Even my leather bike shoes get dry using this approach.

- *Bike selection.* I agree that a fancy bike isn't necessary, but it sure makes riding a lot more fun. Plus, higher-quality equipment (especially gears and brakes) often is more dependable and lasts longer than the cheaper stuff. That being said, I rode a $300 (new cost) bike about 5,000 miles a year for a couple of years as my first commuter here in Memphis. It worked well enough. However, what I have since found is that a bike tailored for the specific person and commute works better and makes for a happier rider. An excellent choice for a lot of urban folks going shorter distances (to me this is less than eight miles) would be a decent mountain bike with slim, high-pressure road slicks, front shock, fenders, and a rear rack for panniers.

- *Be visible.* I ride in the dark with reflective ankle bands, a powerful halogen light (with one battery charger at home and one at the office), an LED headlight, and an LED helmet-mounted light, plus a rear red blinkie and a rear reflective warning triangle. More is better with lights and reflectors.

—Dr. Cliff Heegel, PhD, Memphis, Tennessee

Bike with a Friend

Commuting by bicycle is fun, but it can be even more fun when you get other people involved. Maybe you have a coworker who lives near you or a neighbor who works in the same office building. If you cycle together you can share experiences from the road, swap tips and strategies, and explore new routes. Plus, riding in a group is safer. You could even check with your local bike shop or cycling club to see if you can find a commuting veteran to be your mentor.

Get Ready to Get Healthy

Bicycle commuting for the first time is like starting a new daily exercise routine. If you're already in good physical condition, you should have no problem. But if you've been behind a car steering wheel for so long that your pants no longer fit, you better see a doctor first. Getting a complete physical is a hassle, but it's a worthwhile precaution.

Unless you're an avid weekend cyclist, you may be sore for the first week or so of riding to work. Don't be discouraged. Soreness is a sign that your muscles are growing and getting stronger. Soon that soreness will disappear—along with your love handles!

YOU'D FEEL BETTER ON A BIKE

This text is from the website www.cyclemedia.org, written by Lauren "Dances-with-Cars" Cooper, a bicycle activist living in Carlsbad, California. The excerpt is reprinted with her permission.

Most people can't imagine living without a car, but that's because it's the only thing they've ever known. If I can do it, anyone can. That's one reason I tried it in the first place, to see if an overweight, unathletic, couch potato female could live without a car. First, I love that I don't have to worry about money anymore. I save about $4,000 a year just by not owning an old junker. Whenever I had a car, it always seemed there wasn't enough money. Without a car, it always seems like there's enough, and I even manage to save.

I love that I'm not making children breathe polluted air; and that I don't have to give a weekly allowance to oil tycoons and tyrants, so they have less money to pollute and foul up new places. I love that the money I earn enriches MY bank account instead! Daily bicycling keeps me healthy. I love that I can eat without guilt or worry. No special exercising, no health clubs, no workouts. I love the lessons that bicycling has brought me: self-reliance, patience, the importance of preparation. Bicycling has given me the courage to attempt new, even scary projects. It taught me that, in general, if other people can do something, then I can too; and that the only hard part is thinking about it beforehand. Most people always find excuses; but the bike has taught me that I can always find a way.

I'm in love with something that since 1976 has healed my bad knees, reduced my arthritic hips, lowered my weight, brought me joy, soothed me in sad times, taught me self-discipline, enabled me to be outdoors a lot, helped me stop polluting our earth, and saved me enough money to retire at age thirty-three on a limited income. I'm in love with bicycling for daily transportation.

Most of all, I love the freedom. Freedom from being car-bound my entire life. Freedom from working to "invest" in a car, which loses value yearly. Freedom from poor health, obesity, heart disease, and tiredness. Freedom from sitting in traffic, from being inside a metal crate for hours daily. Freedom to enjoy being outdoors; to enjoy the small adventures encountered on every ride; to ride up a hill and feel stronger at the top; and the freedom of knowing that I can do this every day, for the rest of my life, and it just keeps getting better.

—Lauren Cooper, 52, retired NASA computer programmer

Conquer Your Fears Gradually

Commuting through traffic on a bicycle is a scary concept for some people. If you're apprehensive, don't rush into it. The best way to conquer your fear is to gradually build your cycling skills and your confidence. Start by riding around your neighborhood in the evenings. When you're comfortable with that, move up to cycling along larger streets on the weekends. Eventually you'll have the confidence and skill to handle yourself on a busy thoroughfare at the height of rush hour. Experienced cyclists recommend riding every day to keep skills sharp.

CAR-FREE IN ANN ARBOR, MICHIGAN

I think people think it's attractive—a young woman riding a bike in traffic—it's daring, strong, self-possessed.

—Diana Gavales, 33, graduate student

CHAPTER 14

Walking

*"When I moved a mile away from my job
I lost thirty pounds in nine months."*

—TARA McCOMB, CAR-FREE COMMUTER

According to the 2000 U.S. Census, 3.7 million Americans walk to work. Walking requires no special equipment or training. It's convenient and always available. And it's predictable; there aren't any pedestrian traffic jams, so you always know how long it will take to get to the office.

The only fuel you need to commute on foot is a nutritious breakfast. When you walk to work you won't worry about rising gas prices. Walking is free.

Walking is also the most sustainable form of transportation. It does not cause pollution and has the least impact on the environment. Walking reduces traffic congestion and the need for parking spots. It's also good for you.

The Health Benefits of Walking

The U.S. Surgeon General recommends thirty minutes of exercise a day. Walking to work is a guaranteed way to fit regular exercise into your routine. Daily walking can help you build cardiovascular fitness, control high blood pressure, and decrease the risk of heart disease, stroke, and diabetes. Thirty minutes of walking every day can help lower your cholesterol and reduce your risk of getting cancer. Walking also helps strengthen bones and prevent osteoporosis.

Would you like to lose weight and look great? Walking for thirty minutes a day reduces the risk of obesity. A one-hundred-

and-fifty-pound person will burn roughly one hundred calories per mile of walking. So if you walk two miles each way to the office five days a week, that's two thousand calories you don't have to sweat off on the treadmill. A study by the University of Massachusetts Medical School found that a brisk forty-five-minute walk four times per week for a year could lead to an eighteen-pound weight loss *without dieting*!

Other Benefits of Walking

Many studies link moderate daily exercise, such as walking, to an improved mental outlook and reduced risk of depression and anxiety. People who walk to work say they arrive at the office feeling energized and alert, without an artificial boost from caffeine. Walking every day may even give you more energy and help you sleep better.

Walking to work has social benefits, too. Pedestrian traffic discourages crime and makes citizens feel safer. When you stroll through your community twice a day you'll get to know your neighbors, and you'll meet people on the sidewalk. In contrast, when you drive through your neighborhood in a car you meet no one.

CAR-FREE IN WILMINGTON, NORTH CAROLINA

I save a lot of time living so close to work. Or rather, getting to and from work takes relatively little time, so I have more time before and after work to exercise, cook, relax, read, or hang out with a friend. With a car you think you can and should be able to get a lot done—errands, kids to day care and sports—so you do more and feel busier than you really have to be.

On foot, you can only go at a human pace. You notice more things in your environment: the seasons, the feel and smell of the air, people. I think walking humanizes us. The popular media are full of stories about how busy we are, how stressed and tired, as well as how unhealthy and fat we are. Having a life that is within walking distance is a simple way to counteract that paradigm. I think it is definitely worthwhile to live within walking distance of one's job.

—Elizabeth Peterson, 37, public services librarian

How Far Can You Go?

According to a survey of pedestrians by the U.S. Department of Transportation, the average length of a walking trip is 1.2 miles. For recreational purposes that number climbs to 1.9 miles. Fifteen percent of all walking trips are over 2 miles long. So generally, if you live within 2 miles of work, walking is a realistic mode of commuting.

Living within 2 miles of your workplace also opens up other commuting options. When you're that close, you can in-line skate, skateboard, jog, or ride a push scooter to the office. On a snowy day you could even cross-country ski to work!

Finding the Best Route

As with bicycling, you should try to find two or three different routes to work. You may prefer one route on a calm sunny day, a different route on a windy day, and yet another route if you have to walk home after dark.

THINGS TO LOOK FOR

- Streetlights
- Sidewalks
- Scenic views and tree-lined boulevards
- Proximity to services

CAR-FREE IN BOSTON, MASSACHUSETTS

My husband and I gave up our two cars. We did it because my husband got a job within walking distance of our home. He purposely looked for a job he could walk to because he was sick of commuting an hour and a half every day. He loves walking and his dream of walking to work was fulfilled. To be completely honest, it felt good to be car-free. Eventually we moved to a new home even better situated for car-free living—closer to my school, the metro, and my husband's work. Since that time we never even think about having a car.

—Gabrielle Hermann, 30

THINGS TO AVOID

- Intersections without clearly marked crosswalks
- Loud traffic noise
- Poorly lighted areas
- High crime areas
- Aggressive dogs and heavy-drinking neighbors

Safety

Even though you've been walking your entire life, you still need to take a few precautions when commuting near traffic. First, stay on the sidewalk whenever possible. Where there is no sidewalk, walk *against* oncoming traffic—the opposite is true for bicycling. Use peripheral vision to keep an eye on moving vehicles, and be alert for cars pulling out of driveways, alleys, or side streets.

Second, always cross major streets at a crosswalk; don't jaywalk. When crossing at a busy intersection, beware of drivers making a right turn on red—they're usually looking for cars coming from the left and may not see you. Accept the fact that many drivers do not know pedestrians have the right of way in a crosswalk.

Accept the fact that many drivers do not know pedestrians have the right of way in a crosswalk.

Third, wear light-colored clothing, a reflective vest, or a strobe light when walking in the dark or other poor-visibility conditions. At night carry a flashlight. Use sunscreen in the summer.

Dress for Walking Success

For most of the year you will probably be able to walk to work in regular work clothes. But if it's too hot, wear shorts and a T-shirt during the walk, then change at the office. On chilly mornings, a light jacket is all you'll need because you'll generate body heat as soon as you start walking. And unless there are strong winds, an umbrella will handle the rain. If it's storming, you can either wait it out or wear rain gear as described in chapter 13.

On freezing-cold winter days, dress in layers and wear a wind-blocking nylon shell. Cover exposed skin with gloves, earmuffs, a hat or headband, and a fleece face mask. Dressed properly, I've walked to work in temperatures as low as ten degrees and never felt cold.

All Shoes Are Not Created Equal

Specialized walking shoes are a good idea. Women should not walk to work in high heels; men should not walk in leather dress shoes. Walking shoes are designed specifically to provide much-needed support and cushioning for your feet.

Running shoes are more comfortable than dress shoes, but they don't make ideal walking shoes either. The biomechanics of running differ from walking, therefore shoes for each activity are designed differently. Walking long distances without proper footwear can cause blisters, shin splints, and joint pain.

Most walkers keep a few pair of dress shoes under their desk at work and change out of their walking shoes once they get there. Keep a stash of clean dress socks at work, too, since your feet will sweat during your commute.

Carrying Cargo

A waist pack or small backpack is all you'll need to carry things to and from the office. The best designs transfer most of the weight to a hip belt, so your shoulders don't bear the load. Look for a water-

CAR-FREE IN CAMBRIDGE, MASSACHUSETTS

My husband and I have been car-free for about sixteen years. I chose my current job over another position that paid twice as much because it would allow me to walk to work and the other position would have necessitated a car. Of course it is also delightful to walk, and on the occasions when I am out on the highway during the rush hour I realize how lucky I am. Many people in traditional, not sprawled, communities can easily manage without a car.

—Rosalie Anders, 62

proof or water-resistant material. As with bicycling to work, on a rainy day you may want to wrap your laptop computer, clothes, or other important papers in a plastic trash bag for further protection. I carry a $2,000 Canon digital SLR camera to work in my backpack every day, through rain and snow, and it's never so much as gotten damp.

Getting Started

If you haven't exercised in a while, don't expect to jump right in and walk two miles to work and two miles back. Start slow and ease into it. Perhaps begin by walking for fun on the weekends, then gradually build up to two miles twice a day. Before long you'll be walking to work and back without any problem.

Always consult with a doctor before beginning a new exercise routine. As with any form of exercise, drink plenty of water before, during, and after. A light stretch before each commute is also a good idea.

Walk for the Fun of It

One more benefit of walking to work is that you start and end your day with a fun adventure. You get to feel the change of seasons, enjoy the smell of flowers and cut grass, savor the sunrise, and admire architecture—and you can people-watch. Walking naturally helps you slow down and notice life's little pleasures.

On the way home, walking is a great way to physically relax and mentally de-stress from a day at the office. Driving a car through evening rush hour, however, is an effective way to *increase* your stress level.

CHAPTER 15

Wardrobe, Appearance, and Grooming

"There is no such thing as bad weather,
only inappropriate clothing."

—Sir Ranulph Fiennes, explorer

If you commute by mass transit, motorcycle, scooter, bicycle, or by walking, jogging, or in-line skating, then you're going to be exposed to the weather on your way to work. Wind, rain, and humidity can all take a toll on your clothing, not to mention your hair and makeup. You also might work up a sweat. Because no one wants to spend all day at work looking—or smelling—funky, here are some strategies to help with your wardrobe, appearance, and grooming.

Moderate your exertion level. Regardless of the season or the temperature outside, if you walk, bicycle, or skate to work you can build up a sweat—especially under the arms. So the first strategy is to avoid getting sweaty in the first place by moderating your exertion level on your way to the office. Allow more time, slow your pace, and try to maintain a constant speed. If you feel yourself getting warm or starting to perspire, slow down.

Control your body temperature. You can regulate body temperature by adding or removing layers of clothing. In winter, just removing your hat can help your body cool down rapidly. On really hot summer days it may be a good idea to commute wearing shorts and a T-shirt, then change at work.

Keep dress shoes at the office. Rather than carrying a heavy pair of dress shoes in your backpack every day, keep two or three pairs under your desk at the office. Some women I know keep a dozen pairs of heels under their desk or in a filing cabinet.

Keep a small bag of toiletries in your desk drawer. Stock it with deodorant, a hairbrush, hair spray or gel, toothbrush and toothpaste, a washcloth, spare underwear and dress socks, sunscreen, mouthwash, antibacterial soap, and a towel. Women may want to keep a makeup kit as well.

If your workplace has a shower, keep a shower kit on hand. Be sure it has shampoo, deodorant soap, moisturizer, bath towel, and flip-flops to protect your feet.

Learn to take an instant shower. There are many ways to clean up after arriving at the office sweaty. Here are three that work for me. On days when I just barely break a sweat, I just wait to cool down, then spray on some deodorant. On moderately sweaty days, or if I'm in a hurry, I use antibacterial wet wipes under my arms and on the back of my neck. And on days with heavy perspiration,

CAR-FREE IN CHICAGO, ILLINOIS

Looking professional at the office is not difficult. When I'm working on a day that it has rained or snowed in the morning, none of my coworkers know that I rode my bike to work that day. My first tactic is to ride more slowly. I leave early so that I won't feel a sense of urgency. When I arrive at my office, I take off my helmet and let my hair begin to air-dry. If I'm wearing pants that day, I will lower the pant legs that I had folded up to prevent grease marks or the loose fabric getting caught on the chain of my bike. During this time, my heart rate is settling and my body is cooling off. This process requires just a few minutes.

When I enter the office, I go directly to the restroom, where I have supplies stored. In the bathroom I can remove bike shorts that I am wearing if I am wearing a skirt that day. I keep hair products in the cabinet of the restroom so that I never forget to bring them. On days that it rains, I might wear a raincoat with rain pants, or just the raincoat alone. It is easy to carry a clean bra, panties, and socks in my bag.

Since I bike to work every day all year round, I take this into consideration when I am buying clothes. I wear a synthetic wicking fabric as a base layer. I never wear cotton undergarments because they take forever to dry. I also keep deodorant in my bag and a bottle of essential oil at my desk. This way, if I have to, I can mask any odor with a natural oil scent.

—Anna Glenn, 27, paralegal and graduate student

I go into the restroom with a washcloth and some deodorant soap. I take off my shirt and lather up my underarms, chest, and neck. I rinse out the washcloth, wipe off the soap, blow-dry the wet parts, and spray on some more deodorant. Good as new.

Speed the air-drying process. I keep a blow-dryer at work that has a setting to blow cool air. If I arrive at work wet, I take the blow-dryer into the restroom, point it inside my shirt collar or sleeves, and blow cool air. This evaporates moisture in a minute or two. And I don't even have to take off my shirt.

Avoid helmet head. The hair dryer also helps cure a bad case of helmet head. Most bicycle helmets do not create helmet head because they are vented, so air can blow through and evaporate sweat. Motorcycle helmets, however, tend to hold moisture. If you arrive at work with sweaty, matted helmet hair, grab the blow-dryer from your desk and head straight to the restroom. A few minutes of warm air should restore the body and shape of your hair. If your helmet head is really bad, try wetting your hair in the sink, adding some hair gel, and then blowing it dry.

Keep an entire change of clothes at work. On the rare occasion you get caught in a downpour, you may have to change every item of clothing you're wearing. It's a good idea to keep a complete change of clothes on hand (socks, underwear, belt, and so on), just in case.

Ask about extra storage at work. Many businesses have unused storage space, perhaps in a maintenance room or supply closet. If you can't find any place to put your extra clothing and toiletries at work, ask the custodial staff for suggestions. You can buy a small,

CAR-LITE IN TORONTO, ONTARIO
I do not think sweating is a problem. I know a lot of people view it as insurmountable. On even the hottest days, I sit at my desk, check my morning email, etc., while I stop sweating and cool down (takes ten to fifteen minutes on a very hot day). Then I change into clean, dry clothes, and it's not a problem, and has never been.

—Richard Nelson, 51, management consultant

CAR-FREE IN CHICAGO, ILLINOIS

The foulest weather here is extreme heat and extreme cold. I have a light waterproof, breathable shell jacket for layering over sweaters, and a pair of waterproof, breathable rain pants for rain and snow. Wool and tech fibers are my friends, cotton is not—except on perfect summer days.

I try to ride in my work clothes, but will pack them on the hottest days, or on days I have meetings and need to look spiffy. I think saying you can't ride or walk to work because you don't have showers at the workplace is a silly excuse. Sometimes I just bring a dry wash cloth with some Dr. Bronner's peppermint soap (refreshing) already squirted onto it. If I arrive sweaty, I wet the cloth and wipe off the smelly bits, then reapply deodorant. Most of the time I ride at such a pace that I don't work up a sweat at all.

—Lisa Phillips, project coordinator

locking wardrobe closet from Home Depot for about $50. Put one of these in an out-of-the-way place and your storage problem is solved.

Find a nearby health club. If you intend to jog to work, you'll probably need a full shower before beginning your day. If your workplace doesn't have shower facilities, look for a gym or fitness club nearby. Some health clubs offer locker-room-only memberships at a reduced rate. If you can't find a fitness club near work, perhaps you can walk or take mass transit to work in the morning, then jog home in the evening.

Keep an extra jacket at the office. If the weather turns bad while you're at work, you may need some extra layers for the walk or ride home.

Enlist employer support. Ask the company you work for to install a bike rack, a shower, or some lockers for car-free commuters. Remind your boss of the benefits of commuting to work without a car.

CHAPTER 16

The Trial Run

"Adventure is just bad planning."

—ROALD AMUNDSEN, EXPLORER

After reading chapters 8 through 15, you've probably already identified the mode of car-free commuting that will be the quickest and most convenient for your particular situation. But the fastest way isn't always the best way. Here are nine criteria to keep in mind as you evaluate transportation options:

1. Safety
2. Availability of emergency assistance
3. Reliability
4. Convenience
5. Daily, monthly, and annual costs
6. Accessibility of pick-up and drop-off locations
7. Shelter from inclement weather
8. Proximity to stores, shops, and restaurants
9. Cleanliness

Remember that safety is always the most important criterion. A fast commute may save time, but a safe commute saves lives.

The Weekend Trial Run

Now it's time to give your new commute a try. But rather than risk it on a workday, try it on a weekend. This way if you accidentally take the wrong train, miss your bus stop, or get a flat tire on your bike you won't be late for work. Remember that transit schedules vary on weekends and holidays.

Before you go, tell your family or friends what you're doing. Keep their cell phone numbers handy in case you need assistance. And always have a backup plan—like the phone numbers of local taxi companies—in case you get stranded.

If you're planning to bicycle commute, see if you can get a friend to ride with you on your weekend trial run. It will be more fun, and your friend may notice things along the way that you don't. Plus, you'll feel safer exploring a route through unfamiliar neighborhoods when you're not alone.

Finally, try to make the trial run as close to the real thing as possible. If you plan to ride to work carrying your laptop and lunch in a backpack, do the same thing on your trial run. If you'll be commuting at 7:30 in the morning, make your trial run at the same time of day. If you think you'll take one route on the way to the office and a different one on the way home, mimic that pattern.

Evaluating the Trial Run

After you've made it to work and back once, your confidence will soar—even though you did it on a Saturday morning instead of during rush hour. If things didn't go exactly smoothly during your trial run, you will still feel a sense of accomplishment. And you will have learned from your mistakes. Here are a few questions to ask yourself after completing your weekend trial run:

- Did you feel safe?
- If you had an emergency, would you be able to get help?
- How long did it take from doorstep to doorstep?
- Did you pick the best route?
- Did you get sweaty?
- How much money did you spend?
- Would foul weather pose a problem?
- Are there services along your route that you could use, like a dry cleaner, grocery store, bank, coffee shop, or post office?

Of course, the big question is, can you see yourself commuting this way every day? Remember, it *will* feel different from the way you're used to commuting. It may even feel slower. Car owners often jump to the conclusion that all other modes of local travel are inefficient by comparison. But again, when you commute car-free you save time in other areas.

Becoming a Car-Free Commuter

Once you've made a successful weekend trial run, it's time to put your new commuting plan into daily practice. "But shouldn't I wait until I've made three or four successful weekend commutes?" Dude, this isn't a space shuttle launch. It's just getting to work and back. One successful trial run is all it should take. But do whatever makes you comfortable.

The day you make your first real, weekday car-free commute it's a good idea to leave plenty early. This will allow extra time for traffic and larger crowds, which were probably absent during the weekend run. Again, if it doesn't go perfectly smoothly the first day, don't sweat it. The more you do it, the more efficient your car-free commute will become. Soon you'll have complete confidence in your ability to get to work reliably and on time every day—even in bad weather.

CAR-LITE IN FERGUSON, MISSOURI

I attended a bicycle commuting seminar at an REI store. Then I drove my prospective route. Next I rode it on my bike on a Saturday with my wife driving the car behind, in case I needed assistance. After that, I started riding in and having my wife take me home with the bike on the rack. Eventually I got to riding both directions. I recommend this to anyone who is willing to make a change for the good of themselves and others. It isn't something that happens overnight. It takes planning and education. I especially suggest it for people who live within five miles of work. Which according to statistics is like 50 percent of the people I work with. It really reminds you that every day is a gift . . . that you can accept the status quo (driving a car), or you can go against the stream and make a difference for you and for the entire world.

—Jeff Jackson, 30, banker

Can I Stop Reading Now?

"Now that I can get to work without a car, I know how to live car-free, right?" Not quite. At this point you know enough to live car-lite. But reliable commuting is only *one* essential element of car-free living. Managing your non-work-related transportation is also important. In the next section we'll show you how to run errands, grocery shop, go on dates, and get to every event on your social calendar—all without owning a car.

CAR-FREE IN CHICAGO, ILLINOIS

When my husband and I first moved here, we were paying $235 a month to park our car two blocks from our apartment. We also found that upon moving to Chicago, our car insurance rates increased by 50 percent. Finally, we found that we simply didn't enjoy driving here. We found the traffic frustrating, drivers pushy and prone to honk, and the frequent non-perpendicular intersections tricky to maneuver. So the decision to get rid of the Honda wasn't a tough one. We anticipated saving serious money—around $3,000 a year in parking fees, around $1,400 for insurance, and $2,000 or more yearly for maintenance and gas.

Generally we find commuting and doing errands by foot, mass transit, and bicycle much less of a hassle than by car. We consider the removal of traffic and parking anxiety from our lives to be a huge bonus. We feel, quite literally, "footloose" when we remember we don't have to worry about where we're going to park.

However, one of the biggest drawbacks to not having a car is the ease of getting anywhere on the spur of the moment. With a car, there are no compunctions about heading to Chinatown (eight miles away) for some takeout at ten o'clock at night. So the biggest challenge to not having a car is probably the need for planning. If you want to go somewhere that is too distant to reach on foot or bike, or public transit doesn't serve frequently, it becomes necessary to consult bus and train schedules, organize rides with friends, or rent a vehicle.

In general, it takes us longer to get places by walking, biking, or using public transportation. However, that's time well spent for us. Walking or biking, we're getting some exercise and engaging with our surroundings. On public transit we're typically reading.

—Deb Oestreicher

PART THREE

Non-Work
Transportation

CHAPTER 17

General Strategies for Non-Work Transportation

"An unhurried sense of time is in itself a form of wealth."

—BONNIE FRIEDMAN, AUTHOR

Non-work-related transportation includes things like social-izing, dating, and going furniture shopping, grocery shopping, to the mall, to the drugstore, to the health club, and to your mother-in-law's house for dinner. Important stuff, to be sure. So clearly, if you're going to live well without owning a car, you'll need a way to get your personal stuff done. This chapter offers some overall strategies. The six chapters that follow provide specific tactics for accomplishing everything on your to-do list and getting to every event on your social calendar—all without owning a car.

The American Way: Drive Everywhere (and Spend Money)

I have a female friend who I consider to be a fairly typical Ameri-can car owner. She spends ten to fifteen hours of her free time each week "running errands" in her car. She drives all over town buying things she doesn't need, spending money she can't afford to spend, running errands that are unnecessary, not getting any exercise, and eating unhealthy fast food. Then she arrives home each night wondering why she's broke, overweight, exhausted, and has no free time. Sadly, this has become an accepted—even expected—way of life for millions of Americans.

The automobile has made transportation so immediately available, it has become the primary enabler of America's culture of instant gratification. When we want something, we hop in the car—often on no more than a whim—and drive to get it. "I want it now!" is practically our national anthem. With a constant barrage of advertisements offering "Same day delivery," "No money down," "Ninety days same as cash," and "No payments until 2012," we are accustomed to getting what we want right away.

But at what cost?

Well, for starters, you have to pay for your car, and we've already seen how that alone can drive you to the poorhouse (pun intended). Then you have to pay for all the stuff you keep buying because you drive three times a week to the mall—or as I call it, retail temptation island. When you factor in car loans and easy credit, it's no wonder Americans have the lowest savings rate of any industrialized nation. The average credit card debt per U.S. household is more than $8,000. According to a Federal Reserve study, 43 percent of Americans spend more than they earn. To a large degree those sad statistics stem from America's obsession with the automobile.

Strategy One: Eliminate Unnecessary Trips

The first general strategy for non-work transportation is to eliminate unnecessary trips from your to-do list. Ask yourself, "Do I really need to physically go there?" The answer is usually no; most car trips are unnecessary. Just because you've always accomplished certain tasks by driving doesn't mean that's the only way—or even the best way. In the next chapter we'll show you how virtually all of your errands can come to you.

And here's a built-in bonus. Remember back in chapter 3 how I said automobiles devour so much of our free time? That's partly because owning a car requires you to run *car-related* errands. When you get rid of your car, many of the items that once occupied your to-do list will disappear.

Strategy Two: Walk, Bicycle, or Take Public Transit

According to Investigate Biodiversity, an educational website created by Conservation International and Intel Corporation, "Eighty percent of all car trips in the United States are within eight miles of home, a very doable bike ride. Forty percent of car trips are two miles or less." Does eight miles seem too far for a bike ride? Does two miles seem too far to walk? Try it; you might be surprised by just how easy it is. And when you combine public transit and riding your bicycle, you should be able to get almost anywhere in the city.

Strategy Three: Find Closer Alternatives

For destinations that are too far to walk or pedal to, consider replacing them with options that are closer to home. This may require some research and force you to change long-standing habits. For example, for years I went to the same Catholic church out of habit, even though it was miles away. When I decided to go car-free I researched alternatives. It turned out there were two other Catholic churches within two miles of my house. Actually, one was less than a half mile away, yet I never noticed it until I started actively looking for a closer alternative.

I used this same strategy to find a closer hair salon, gym, library, department store, drug store, doctor, dentist, bank, deli, and bookstore—all within a short walk, bicycle ride, or transit ride from my home. I even found a nearby homeless shelter where I do

CAR-FREE IN CAMBRIDGE, MASSACHUSETTS

Living car-free means sometimes you have to plan! I know Americans want 24/7 access to everything, and that the concept of planning ahead is outrageous. But what people don't seem to understand is that *not* planning requires them to spend so much more time, energy, and money on things that actually make them *less* free in other ways. So a big challenge is to personally come to terms with planning ahead, being flexible, and occasionally being inconvenienced—in order to access the big picture of overall more life freedom.

—Jeffrey Rosenblum, 37, consultant

volunteer work. Once you begin actively looking closer to home, you will be amazed by the options that are available.

Strategy Four: Plan Ahead and Stock Up

When you own a car, you really don't have to plan much. If you're doing laundry and you run out of fabric softener, you can just drive to the convenience store during the rinse cycle. But when you live car-free it's not that simple.

Living without a car requires you to think ahead and seize opportunities to stock up. For example, when your car-owning neighbor invites you to go on a run to Sam's Club, your buying habits will be different than his. He'll probably buy just one box of Cheerios, but you'll buy two or three because you're not sure when you'll get back to Sam's. You'll also take a few minutes to think ahead to any holidays and birthdays coming up in the next three months, then buy greeting cards and supplies accordingly. This will save you from making a separate trip to the store for every occasion, the way most car owners do.

Strategy Five: Be Creative and Stay Flexible

Even though this country was built around the automobile, you can still access all of its features without owning one. A little creativity is usually all it takes.

Can't get to the bank? You can now do almost all of your banking by mail, online, or through an automated teller machine. You can even buy stamps and traveler's checks at an ATM. Can't find good fresh produce in your neighborhood? Stock up on frozen goods. Out-of-town friends or relatives coming for a visit? Rent a car for the weekend. If it's summertime, rent a convertible! In years of living without a car I have yet to find a situation that could not be solved with a little flexibility and creativity. See chapter 23 for more on this topic.

CAR-FREE IN CHICAGO, ILLINOIS

It takes a while to learn a different way of doing things. When I was driving daily and my car would break down everything seemed like a challenge because I didn't know any other way. Now that I'm living car-free it doesn't seem like a challenge at all. If it did I'd resume driving. I've found better ways of doing everything that I previously did by car.

—Todd Allen, 40, computer programmer

CHAPTER 18

Make Your Errands Come to You

"Nothing is stronger than habit."

—Ovid

Virtually any errand and almost all shopping can be done easily and conveniently without ever getting into a car. First, try shopping locally by riding your bike or walking to nearby stores. Patronizing neighborhood businesses keeps local economies strong and leads to social interaction within the community. But if your neighborhood doesn't have merchants that carry what you need, it's time to get online.

The Internet has revolutionized the way we conduct business, communicate, research products, and shop. There is seldom any reason to actually visit a big-box retail store these days, let alone an entire strip mall. In this chapter you'll find some ideas to get you started shopping and running errands from home.

The Problem with Car-Based Errands

Car owners generally run errands by driving. They drive to the bank, to the post office, to the drug store, to the fabric store, and even to the health club. They circle the mall looking for parking, then wait with their blinker on for someone to vacate a spot. They leave the mall two hours later and spend more time searching for their car. They arrive home that evening having spent three hours of their life "running errands."

Plus they spent $10 on gas, $5 on food, and who knows how much on impulse buys. They also risked serious injury fighting other cars and SUVs in highway traffic.

There Is a Better Way

If there were no other way to accomplish the tasks required for everyday life, we could justify such a system of car-based errands. But all that driving is unnecessary, not to mention a tremendous waste of time and energy. Unless your errands include something out of the ordinary—like providing a urine sample or a medical appointment that requires you to be there in person—they can probably be done from your home or office computer. Below is a list of errands that car owners would typically drive to to accomplish. Yet every one of these can easily be taken care of from home in a matter of minutes.

- Renting videos or DVDs
- Going to the drugstore
- Shopping for electronics
- Buying stamps at the post office
- Dropping off film to be developed
- Picking up a prescription at the pharmacy
- Depositing a check at the bank
- Picking up clothes at the dry cleaner
- Buying groceries
- Shipping a package
- Taking a computer in for repairs
- Going to night school to earn a college degree

CAR-FREE IN SANTA BARBARA, CALIFORNIA

I do all banking and bill paying online, even the rent. That really frees up the schedule. I also have online access to all the digital databases and electronic journals through the UCSB library. Electronic access to a university library allows me to do quality research (including document retrieval) right from home, on my own time. As for shopping, when I buy big items I have them delivered. My desk, bookshelves, lamps, kitchenware, comforter, and more, they all came from online retailers via UPS or some other delivery service. And that reminds me, DHL and UPS all come right to your door, same-day service when it's time to send a package. Why drive to them?

—Scott M. Lacy, PhD, 35, anthropologist

The biggest obstacle for most car owners is breaking the ingrained habit of using the car to accomplish every errand. It may feel a bit odd when you first sit down at the computer to shop for toothpaste. But when it arrives at your doorstep a few days later—with *free shipping*—you'll recognize the beauty of buying from home.

Online Grocery Shopping

One of the first questions people ask when I tell them I don't own a car is, "How do you buy groceries?" Most people are so car-centered in their thinking they can't imagine any other way than by driving to the supermarket. My response to that question is standard: "I stock up on nonperishables at Sam's Club every couple of months; I buy milk, bread, and fresh produce at local stores in my neighborhood; and I have groceries delivered to my doorstep. There's no reason to go to the supermarket anymore."

Most major regional supermarket chains offer online grocery shopping with door-to-door delivery. Just call the large supermarkets in your area and ask, or visit their websites and click on "services." Many smaller supermarkets and neighborhood grocers also deliver. An easy way to research this is to do a Google search under "[your city]"+"online grocery shopping." If that doesn't work, try "[your city]"+"grocery delivery."

There will be an additional charge for delivery. But remember what you're actually saving. When you add up the time it would take to drive to the supermarket, wander the aisles, wait in line to check out, load the groceries into your car, then drive home, plus the money you'd spend on gas and on impulse purchases, paying the delivery fee starts to look like a bargain.

Another home delivery option is NetGrocer (www.netgrocer .com). This is a national company that ships nonperishable food (plus drugstore items, pet food, and thousands of other products) directly to your doorstep. NetGrocer serves all fifty states and they use FedEx delivery, so no signature is required. That means they can leave your order on your doorstep even if you're not home.

One of the benefits of online grocery shopping is the ability to keep your personal shopping list on file. So the next time you're ready to shop, all you have to do is log in, call up your previous shopping list, then click on the items you want to reorder. This saves a tremendous amount of time.

Many online grocers, including NetGrocer, also allow you to set up a "recurring order." This feature will automatically ship your favorite products at time intervals that you specify without your having to do anything. So just when you're about to run out of Lucky Charms and soy milk, they magically appear on your doorstep. This feature takes a little trial and error to get the timing right, but it can be a worthwhile convenience.

Distance Learning

If you plan to earn a college diploma or a graduate degree, you no longer have to drive to campus and sit in class. Most major universities now offer online degree programs, usually called "distance learning." But be careful in researching distance learning institutions, because many are not accredited. Your first step should probably be to visit the websites of the major universities in your area to see if they offer fully accredited distance learning programs.

Dry Cleaning and Laundry

Many dry cleaners now offer pick-up and delivery service to help their busy customers. Some don't even charge an extra fee. Since most dry cleaners don't have fancy websites, the only way to find out which ones offer this service in you area is to make a few phone calls. If you can't find one near your home, try looking for one that will pick up and deliver to your office.

Renting Movies

There's no longer any reason to drive to the video store on a Friday night and pick through what's left of the new releases. The website www.netflix.com changed the way America rents movies; now

Blockbuster, Wal-Mart, and other companies offer similar services. Not only will they mail your DVD rentals right to your home or office, they'll also provide you with prepaid return envelopes. Shipping is free both ways. And there's another bonus: no late fees.

You can browse tens of thousands of titles online and set up your own favorite movies list. These services make money by charging a flat monthly fee. Plans start at around $10 per month, but most customers opt for the unlimited rental plans, for around $18 per month. I used to pay more than that just in late fees!

Film Developing

Whether you shoot film or digital, there's no reason to drive to the mall to drop off your images for developing or printing. Digital files can be uploaded to any number of photo-processing websites. Then you can order prints, which will show up a few days later in your mailbox. Some of the most popular photo websites are www .snapfish.com, www.shutterfly.com, www.ezprints.com, www.fuji-film.net, and www.kodakgallery.com. If you shoot film, you can mail your rolls to these companies and have the digital files posted in an online gallery, as well as get prints mailed to you.

Online Drugstores

Online drugstores like www.walgreens.com, www.cvs.com, and www.drugstore.com have tens of thousands of products conveniently grouped into categories like: health, personal care, hair care, pharmacy, beauty, skin care, vitamins, diet and fitness, men's grooming, and so on. And most orders qualify for free shipping.

I have done price comparisons and found that—for the products I buy—Drugstore.com prices are about the same as at my local Walgreens. When Drugstore.com has a sale or a special offer their prices are usually lower. All of the online drugstores seem to be very good about informing me via email when the items on my shopping list go on sale.

Find Your Own Favorites

Whatever errands you typically run, whatever your hobby is, whatever you want to buy, whatever you're passionate about, you will find a website that focuses on it. Whether you collect rare cognac or grow exotic orchids, you'll find a retailer online.

My hobby is digital landscape photography, and I have found literally dozens of websites devoted to this interest. In the past year I've purchased more than $3,000 worth of camera equipment, batteries, books, software, lenses, and filters, yet I never had to set foot in a car.

CHAPTER 19

The Miracle of Car Sharing

"It's as easy as getting cash from an ATM."

—Zipcar, car-sharing company

If you've learned to commute to work without a car, eliminate unnecessary trips, find closer alternatives, and make your errands come to you, you're 99 percent of the way to living well without owning a car. But there are still some things that are best accomplished by driving a motor vehicle. Whether you need to haul firewood (many firewood sellers deliver, by the way) or move a couch, for certain tasks it's more convenient to use a car, truck, or minivan. In these cases, car sharing is the perfect solution. With car sharing you get to *use* a car without the costs and responsibilities of *owning* one.

Exponential Growth

Car-sharing companies have found a fast-growing niche. Their market is city dwellers who are tired of the expense and headache of owning a car but still occasionally want to use one. According to the U.S. Transportation Research Board, "Car sharing has experienced exponential growth." Car sharing began in 1998 in three U.S. cities; there is now some form of car sharing in nearly forty U.S. cities. In 2000 there were only six car-sharing organizations in this country; there are now more than fifteen in the U.S. and eleven in Canada.

Boston-based Zipcar is the largest U.S. car-sharing company, with more than 55,000 members and an average of 1,250 new members signing up each month. As this book goes to press, Zipcar operates in Boston, Washington, D.C., San Francisco, UNC

Chapel Hill, Minneapolis, Toronto, and New York. Zipcar plans to expand to twenty-five additional U.S. cities in the next five years, including Atlanta, Austin, Chicago, Dallas, Miami, Philadelphia, Phoenix, Pittsburgh, Portland, Seattle, and Vancouver.

According to Zipcar's corporate marketing manager, Colleen Woods Heikka, "Now that we've established profitability and built an incredibly loyal and enthusiastic member base, we are able to make the necessary investments to launch Zipcar as a national brand. Our goal is to create what does not yet exist, the first nationwide car-sharing company."

"Seattle-based Flexcar sold majority control last month to an investment group led by America Online founder Steve Case and legendary auto executive Lee Iacocca. Zipcar in Cambridge, Mass., landed $10 million in venture funding in July led by Benchmark Capital, a Silicon Valley firm whose previous investments include eBay."

—*USA Today*, SEPTEMBER 15, 2005

Flexcar is the other large car-sharing company in the U.S. As this book goes to press, Flexcar operates in Seattle, Portland, Los Angeles, San Francisco, San Diego, Washington, D.C., and Chicago.

How Car Sharing Works

Car-sharing organizations keep a fleet of cars and light trucks in parking spots scattered around a city. Members make reservations by calling a toll-free number or by using a website or other wireless technology—anywhere from one minute to one year in advance. Members then just walk to the car they reserved, access it with an electronic keycard, and drive away.

When they're finished using it, members return the car to the same parking spot. Drivers don't directly pay for gas, insurance, taxes, registration, parking, or maintenance. Instead, car-sharing members typically pay a flat hourly fee, a per-mile rate, and a monthly membership fee.

Drivers can usually apply for a membership in a matter of minutes online. You must be twenty-one or older, have a valid driver's license, and meet certain safe-driving standards. Once approved, members have access to a fleet of vehicles ranging from economy cars and hybrids to BMWs, Mini Coopers, convertibles, and pickup trucks. All vehicles are vacuumed, washed, and serviced on a regular basis.

CAR-FREE IN WASHINGTON, D.C.

Since I take the Metro to work (it's faster door to door than driving, and cheaper than paying to park in the garage), I only ever need a car evenings and weekends. When you calculate the cost of owning a car that you only use maybe once or twice a week, it just doesn't make sense. Plus, my car got broken into, someone bumped it while it was parked, it needed new tires, and whenever I went out of town for work or vacation, I had to find someone to move it all the time. So getting rid of it felt like the sensible thing to do. And it was actually a liberating experience! Not to mention all that extra $$ in my pocket.

Then I joined Zipcar. There were Zipcars all over my neighborhood, often closer than any space I could ever find for my own car, so it seemed pretty convenient. I use Zipcar mostly for those random last-minute things. The other day I had to bring a big box to the post office and it was raining—there was a Honda Element less than two blocks away, and in an hour I returned it, which cost me about half what a taxi would. I like picking people up at the airport and impressing them with a BMW—even three hours of Zipcar rental is cheaper than the airport shuttle. Once I forgot something at work and zipped back to the office in a Prius. (When you use a Zipcar you call it "zipping.")

There are even Zipcars near work, too, so if I need to run an errand during my lunch hour, it's no problem. I have a friend who uses Zipcar to drive back home and walk his dog during the day, which is cheaper than hiring a dog walker. It's just so much cheaper. When I need a car for a couple days or a week at a time, then I rent one from Avis or Hertz, and get a great deal online . . . gotta pay for gas though; that stinks.

—Aurelie Shapiro, 27, oceanographer

On-Demand Transportation without the Hassle

The ease of use and booming growth of car sharing is making car ownership seem almost outdated in many urban areas. Car sharing transforms automobiles from a product to a service. Members get all the benefits of using a car without the hassles of owning one.

Car sharing makes accessing a vehicle twenty-four hours a day as easy as withdrawing money from an ATM. And unlike renting a car, there is no time-consuming paperwork or in-person check-in process. Many car-sharing customers say they use car sharing when they need the car for only a few hours, or when they need a car on the spur of the moment; they use a traditional rent-a-car when they need a vehicle for a few days or longer.

Another benefit of car sharing is that you get to choose the most appropriate vehicle for the job. If you're hauling plywood, reserve the pickup truck or minivan. If you're driving by yourself to grandma's house, get the hybrid. And if you're taking your date to a black-tie gala, go for the BMW.

Car sharing is also a natural solution for parents with young children. It's perfect for trips to the doctor, once-a-week piano lessons, and the occasional last-minute run to the drugstore. If your children can get to school without your having to drive them, car

CAR-FREE IN CAMBRIDGE, MASSACHUSETTS

When we calculated how much we were spending on our car and how much gas it guzzled, we decided to experiment with not using the car at all for about three weeks and see if it was manageable. We noticed that even in the coldest winter weather, we lived just as comfortably without a car. This is when Doug signed up for Zipcar. There are about four Zipcars that we can easily walk to around our neighborhood. We use Zipcar to run errands such as grocery shopping and going to the hardware store. We no longer have to worry about finding parking around town. We no longer worry about street cleaning. Street cleaning required us to park on the even side of the street on one day and on the odd side the next day. The benefits of car sharing via Zipcar are countless. We do not miss having a car, and we love our car-free and car-sharing life.

—Doug and Patricia Seidler, 30 and 27, architect and schoolteacher sharing may be able to fill in the rest of the transportation gaps. Then instead of spending money on owning a car you can invest it in a college fund.

Financial Benefits of Car Sharing

The most obvious benefit of replacing car ownership with car sharing is the cost savings. With car sharing the costs of ownership and maintenance are spread among thousands of members. Plus, you only pay for what you use. According to a survey by City Car Share in the San Francisco Bay Area, members spent an average of $540 per year on car sharing. A survey of Zipcar members found that they saved an average of $5,232 per year by using car sharing.

Other Benefits

Studies show that each vehicle in a car-sharing fleet replaces between ten and twenty cars on the road. According to car-sharing company CommunAuto, 26 percent of members have given up a car, and 58 percent have avoided buying a car since they joined. Zipcar estimates that its service has taken twelve thousand privately owned vehicles off the road.

Car-sharing members also drive less than car owners. A recent survey found that before joining Zipcar members drove an average of 5,295 miles per year. After joining, they drove an average of 369 miles per year.

Fewer cars on the road and less driving lead to reduced traffic congestion, lower tailpipe emissions, reduced need for parking spots and parking garage construction, lower overall expenditure on transportation, and more efficient use of land and other resources.

CAR-SHARING WEBSITES

www.zipcar.com
www.flexcar.com
www.citycarshare.org
www.carsharing.net
www.innovativemobility.org
www.communauto.com (Canada)
www.communitycar.com (Madison, Wisconsin)

Land that might have been used for the construction of a multilevel concrete parking garage can instead be used for parks, green space, or affordable housing.

According to a report published by City Car Share, "Car sharing brings a broad range of social and environmental benefits for members, non-members, and the wider community. In short, it can help make communities more vibrant, attractive, and less dependent on the private automobile, and contribute to a range of transportation, housing, economic development, and social justice goals."

If the city where you live does not have car sharing, chances are good that it will soon. Major national expansions by Flexcar and Zipcar—fueled by corporate investment—are under way in many cities as this book goes to print. There are also small, community-based car-sharing co-ops popping up all over the country. To find out if your city has a car-sharing program, visit the websites listed on page 165. Or do a Google search by typing "car sharing"+"[your city]."

CHAPTER 20

Rental Car Weekends

"Never measure the height of a mountain until you have reached the top. Then you will see how low it was."

—Dag Hammarskjöld, former Secretary-General of the United Nations

If car sharing is not available in your area, occasionally renting a car is a convenient alternative. As discussed in the previous chapter, there are certain tasks that are best accomplished by driving a motor vehicle—especially moving heavy loads or traveling beyond the reach of public transit. Renting a car may also be worthwhile when you have friends or family coming in from out of town and you'll need to chauffeur them around.

Weekend Rentals

I recommend renting cars on a weekend for a couple of reasons. First, weekend rentals are cheaper. Most car rental companies offer discounted in-town weekend rates, sometimes as low as $9.99 to $19.99 per day, depending on where you live. So from Friday through Sunday your total bill with taxes and surcharges might be less than $60. This low rate usually does not include unlimited mileage or out-of-state travel. But it allows plenty of mileage for running errands and visiting people. And here's an insider's tip: if you can't get a special weekend rate, then pick up the car on Saturday morning and return it first thing Monday morning. That way you get practically the whole weekend with the car but you pay for only two days.

The second reason to rent a car on the weekend is that you can get more done—assuming Saturday and Sunday are your days off work. I save up errands over a period of months, then rent a car and get them all done in a single weekend. Along with making trips to the shopping center, the home improvement store, and Sam's Club, I'll also plan visits with friends who live out in the suburbs or other distant areas.

Planning Is Important

The best way to make the most of your rental car weekends is to plan them well in advance. I find it helpful to keep a running list of everything I want to accomplish the next time I rent a car. Then a few days before the rental car weekend, I'll create a rough itinerary so I can maximize my efficiency in the forty-eight hours I have the car. You'll be amazed at how much you can get done in two days with a little preplanning and organization.

It's also a good idea to schedule your rental car weekends to coincide with events on your social calendar. For example, if you know you'll have to drive to a friend's graduation ceremony in early May, plan that as your rental car weekend. That way you can get all your shopping and errands done on Saturday and go to the graduation on Sunday.

Here is a list of things to consider putting on your to-do list for every rental car weekend:

- Bulk shopping at Sam's Club or Costco
- Shopping for bulky home improvement items or furniture (rent a truck or van)

CAR-FREE IN SANTA BARBARA, CALIFORNIA

When I want one, I rent a car. I always get a new car, and when I turn it back in, that's it! No more worries about insurance, maintenance, etc. Truly a great short-term relationship.

—Garrick Sitongia, 43, electrical engineer

- Moving anything large or heavy
- Making merchandise returns
- Taking something to be repaired
- Visiting friends or relatives
- Shopping at specialty stores that can't be reached by bicycle or transit
- Shopping for clothing that you must try on for proper fit

Pick Enterprise—They'll Pick You Up

I've used all of the major rental car companies, and all can offer competitive rates and excellent service. But I recommend Enterprise Rent-A-Car (www.enterprise.com) for several reasons. First, their customer service is excellent. Second, they take care of their frequent customers, often providing free upgrades and special deals, like unlimited mileage. Third, they send out email specials with coupons that offer their best rates. Fourth, while Hertz and Avis primarily target the airport business, Enterprise has focused on opening multiple locations throughout each city to facilitate what they call "neighborhood" rentals. In fact, Enterprise has 6,500 locations, more than any other rental car agency. According to their website, "Enterprise has locations within 15 miles of 90 percent of the U.S. population." So there's probably one near you. And most important, an Enterprise employee will actually pick you up at home or at work and drop you off at no extra charge. This is a tremendous convenience for anyone living car-free.

CAR-FREE IN SALT LAKE CITY, UTAH

On occasion when I need a car, I walk two blocks to Enterprise Rent-A-Car. Their weekend deal, for a compact car, is only $9.99 (plus tax) per day. Having a car rental location in my neighborhood provides a safety net for those unforeseen emergencies or weekend trips. An Enterprise employee even drives me to work on Monday morning after I return the car.

—Julie Bond, 40, regional marketing specialist

Use the Right Credit Card

Some credit cards offer a collision damage waiver (CDW) program. This feature means the credit-card company provides insurance coverage for any damage done to a rental car. If you pay for the rental with a credit card that offers a CDW program you may be able to decline the rental car company's very expensive collision insurance. Contact your credit-card provider or review your credit-card agreement to see if you have this coverage. It can save you between ten and twenty dollars a day when renting a car. Caution: make sure you read the fine print so you know exactly what's covered and what isn't. And be sure to bring a copy of the CDW to the rental company's office; they may ask to see it.

How Often?

In your first few months of living car-free you may find yourself renting a car once a month. But as you become more experienced at living without a car you'll find other ways to do the things that you used to accomplish by driving. Soon you'll rely on renting cars less and less. Eventually, renting a car once every three to six months will probably be enough. Many car-free people never rent cars. But in the beginning, renting is a great way to ease the transition to a car-free lifestyle.

CAR-FREE IN CHICAGO, ILLINOIS

We do rent a car on Thanksgiving so we can hit both families' turkey dinners on the same day. We rent a car on some out-of-town vacations, too. The most recent rental was seven months ago—we rented a cargo van so we could pick up a couch in Wisconsin that I bought on eBay.

—Rochelle Cohen Loder, 38, scientific copy editor

CHAPTER 21

Friends, Relatives, and Coworkers

*"Go through your phone book, call
people and ask them to drive you to the
airport. The ones who will drive you
are true friends. The rest aren't bad
people; they're just acquaintances."*

—Jay Leno, comedian

Don't expect this or rely on it, but in practice, friends, family members, and coworkers who own cars often become a source of ad hoc transportation for people who live car-free. They know many of the same people you do, and they're often going to the same places. Who better to give you a ride?

Once your car-owning friends learn you no longer have a car, you'll be surprised how frequently they invite you to go with them to the mall or grocery store. The key to accepting these offers without guilt—and without taking advantage—is to make sure that each ride you accept is a win-win for you and the driver. Think of it as a form of impromptu, informal carpooling—they drive, and you help pay the cost of gas and parking.

Shared Transportation: A Win-Win

When it comes to accepting rides, you must remember one important law of human interaction: people like helping others, but they resent feeling that someone is taking advantage of them. Always make sure the driver knows how much you appreciate his help. Words are a good start, but actions speak louder. Below are some thoughtful ways to make your friends and family glad they gave you a ride. Any one item from the list below should do the trick.

- Always say a sincere "Thank you!"
- Offer to pay for parking
- If you go shopping together, treat the driver to lunch
- Fill up their tank or chip in for gas
- Pay for an automatic car wash
- Check the oil and wash the car windows when you stop for gas

Try these suggestions and you'll quickly see how a little sincere gratitude goes a long way. And you'll be astonished at how willing people are to take you places, so long as they feel appreciated. Just don't go overboard; you don't want anyone to feel obligated to drive you.

"No use earning karma points by giving up your car and then using them right up by demanding people drive you everywhere."

—Patricia Collins, 30, NEVER OWNED A CAR

Bonus: More Time with Friends and Family

When you live car-free you don't *rely* on other people for rides. Rather, you proactively seek group activities and shared transportation. So another potential benefit is that you might spend more time with the people you care about. This can lead to deeper friendships, closer relationships with coworkers, and connections with new people.

CAR-FREE IN WASHINGTON, D.C.

My friends will often offer to give me a ride to an event we are both going to. I don't think they mind, especially since I offer to pay for gas (or buy the first round). And I never take their generosity for granted. Even if none of my friends were able to give me a ride, I could still rent a car without any problem and go to those few events that take me beyond the Metro. Always have a plan B.

—Heidi Deutsch, 31, public health program manager

CHAPTER 22

Socializing and Dating without a Car

> *"Not having a car has improved my social life considerably. I am somewhat of an introvert, but without a car I spend more time with my friends and meet new people all the time. It is awesome!"*
>
> —PETERSON TOSCANO, CAR-FREE COMMUTER

Most of us grew up relying on cars to get us to social events—to school dances, parties, movies, concerts, and everyplace in between. So it's not surprising that as adults we assume a car is essential to an active social life. It isn't.

Without the financial drain of owning a car, you'll have more discretionary cash pumping through your social system. And without the demands of car ownership, you may even have more free time. That means more time and money for lunches with friends, weekend getaways, cocktail parties, dates, and dinners out.

Plan Your Way to Social Success

After you get rid of your car you can still go to all the social functions, activities, and get-togethers that you do now. But unlike when you own a car, you'll have to think about your transportation ahead of time. When you have a car parked outside you can wait until the last minute to decide if you're going to the company picnic. But without a car you'll need to plan a few days in advance. The following is a list of common social activities and some creative car-free ideas for getting to and from each.

BAR HOPPING AND NIGHTCLUBBING

You have several transportation options for this type of socializing. The first—and perhaps safest—is to take a taxi. Bar hopping and clubbing usually involve drinking, so it's often better to take a taxi even if you do own a car.

Another option is to ask one member of the group you'll be going out with to swing by and pick you up. Offer a small incentive, like agreeing to pay the driver's cover charge and buy him a drink at the club.

A third strategy is to influence the choice of the bar. If you can convince your friends to meet at a bar near your home you won't have to drive. Another possibility is to suggest meeting at your place for cocktails before going out. Then you'll have your choice of rides.

The only absolute rule for car-free clubbing and bar hopping is to make sure you always keep enough cash for a taxi ride home—just in case your other options disappear.

SPORTING EVENTS AND CONCERTS

Thanks to thoughtful urban planners, every professional sports stadium and most major concert venues are served by public transit. This is often the best way to get to the game—whether you own a car or not—because you avoid traffic jams and parking hassles. Also, many bars and restaurants offer free shuttle buses to and from ball games.

CAR-FREE IN CHICAGO, ILLINOIS

The best part is that my social life has improved since I've stopped driving. Now that parking and traffic are no longer concerns, I do a lot more things throughout the city. There are occasional events in distant suburbs that can be harder to attend than if I drove. But anything that I've ever really wanted to do I've always found a way. I spend a lot more time socializing and involved in group activities since I've stopped driving. Driving is a fairly solitary activity.

—Todd Allen, 40, computer programmer

RELIGIOUS SERVICES

Many churches, temples, and other places of worship offer shuttle or van service to help members get to services. Simply call the office and inquire. Or, as church or temple members often live in nearby neighborhoods, finding someone to carpool with should not be difficult. Tack a notice on the bulletin board or place an ad in the weekly newsletter. And since you can dress casual at many religious services, riding a bicycle may be an option.

LUNCH AND DINNER DATES

The key here is to influence the day, time, and location of the lunch or dinner, and then meet your date at the restaurant. If there are suitable restaurants near your office, try to schedule a lunch or an early dinner on a workday. If there are restaurants close to your home, schedule a dinner date for later in the evening or on a weekend. If there are no restaurants close to work or home, suggest meeting at one that's easy for you to get to by bike or one that's close to a transit stop.

HOLIDAY OFFICE PARTIES AND COMPANY PICNICS

Any event that is sponsored by your employer or involves many of the people you work with should be easy to get to without a car. A week or so before the event, begin inquiring who's planning to attend. Then ask if you can carpool. Be sure to offer to split the cost of gas and parking. Many employers sponsor "care cabs" or van rides for employees after holiday parties and other official company events where drinking may be involved.

FUNDRAISERS AND CHARITY BENEFITS

Many fundraisers are held at large venues like museums, concert halls, zoos, hotels, and public parks, most of which are served by public transit. If it's a fancy black-tie event you could rent a limousine for the evening and split the cost with a few other couples. Or if the event is being held at a hotel, call the front desk, tell them what event you're coming to, and request the hotel shuttle to pick you up at home. Be sure to tip the driver. Or plan a rental car weekend around a major charity event or social function, then rent a fancy car.

FAMILY GATHERINGS AND HOLIDAYS

Thanksgiving dinner wouldn't be any fun if you were stuck at home while everyone else was gorging on turkey at Grandma's house. Luckily, family functions are among the easiest gatherings to get to. You know everyone who's going, so you know whom to call to arrange a carpool. Or you can eliminate the need to travel altogether by offering to host the family dinner, picnic, party, barbecue, or Monopoly game at your place.

Car-Free Dating and Romance

Because dating in this country is traditionally done in cars, you might worry that your love life will shrivel up and blow away if you don't own one. But that's not going to happen. On the contrary, when you live car-free the opposite sex will consider you interesting, unusual, maybe even mysterious. You'll begin to notice potential partners trying to "figure you out." And a bed of mystery makes fertile soil for romance to bloom. The remainder of this chapter offers combat-tested techniques for maintaining an active dating life without maintaining a personal vehicle.

NOT GENDER-SPECIFIC

Some readers may argue that men are the ones who usually do the driving on dates, so car-free dating will be more difficult for

CAR-FREE IN SAN FRANCISCO, CALIFORNIA

Car-free socializing works very well in San Francisco. I bike to clubs, parties, restaurants. Sometimes I take transit as well. The train is *very* convenient. Caltrain has provided bike cars that hold sixteen or thirty-two bikes depending on model. I and many other bikers use them daily. We even have a weekly party on the bike car (www.partycar.com).

—Amandeep Jawa, 36, software engineer

men than for women. Although this assumption may be true in many cases, this book takes a unisex approach. The suggestions and strategies outlined in this chapter are applicable to men *and* women. If women have it a little easier due to cultural traditions, so be it. But the author must assume that in the new millennium in this country a person of either gender may invite someone (of either gender) on a date. So throughout this book the pronouns *he* or *him* and *she* or *her* are used only for brevity; they are not meant to be gender-specific.

FIRST AND SECOND DATE STRATEGIES

So you meet someone you're interested in, you exchange phone numbers, and now you're ready to ask for that all-important first date. But if you've recently joined the ranks of the car-free, you'll probably worry what the person will think about your not owning a car.

First, relax. This is going to be much easier than you think. There are actually a couple things working in your favor at this point. Number one, on a first date it's perfectly acceptable (even

"I'VE FOUND A SURE WAY TO ATTRACT MEN. I SPRAY NEW CAR SCENT ON MYSELF! I GET DATES AND IT MASKS ANY ODOR OF REALITY!"

preferred) to meet your date at an agreed-upon location instead of traveling there together. "Let's have lunch at TGI Friday's. Shall we meet there around one o'clock?"

Many people feel more comfortable meeting in a public place, especially when it's someone they hardly know. And if you arrange to meet your date at the restaurant, there's no need to discuss your choice of transportation ahead of time. You can keep that information to yourself for the time being. Or share it up front; the choice is yours.

The second thing working in your favor is the natural bonding that takes place when two people spend time together. Before the first date, you are an unknown quantity. But after the first date you have begun to get to know each other on a personal level. So when you discuss your car-free lifestyle, your date will know you better and be inclined to understand. If someone has already started to like you as a person, not owning a car shouldn't be an obstacle to getting additional dates.

CAR-FREE IN LOS ANGELES, CALIFORNIA

I think being car-free has affected my social life positively. I am more fit than most people half my age. I've interacted socially with my community more as I run into more people on bike than I would have in a car.

Sometimes I am slightly apprehensive about telling a woman who I don't know well that I don't drive, but 99 percent of the time when I explain things they understand. Generally on a first or second date, we meet up somewhere—that's easy, I just bike or bus it there. This includes doing things like meeting for dinner, movies, museums, readings, walks, parties, Frisbee in the park, etc.

From there it depends more on the person I am dating. Some women have no interest in doing anything without a car. This isn't my preference, but it works OK. I will bike over to her place, or she will swing by and get me on the way somewhere. When we get gas, I pay to fill her tank.

Los Angeles has hundreds of thousands of people without cars (I've heard it estimated at four hundred thousand). If you think about dates, you don't spend that much time in the car anyway. I don't think it's a problem. If a woman is interested in me, it's because of who I am, not how I get around.

—Joe Linton, 41, artist-designer

Below is a list of car-free first and second date strategies. Experience will teach you which one to use in which situation and with which person.

"Let's meet there." As discussed above, this is a perfectly acceptable way to arrange a first, second, or even a third date. This strategy works for restaurants, coffee shops, jazz clubs, sporting events, movies, and many other types of location-specific dates.

Invite her to your house for dinner. If you can cook, you're golden. When you invite someone to your home for dinner, it's understood that she's going to drive herself there (and probably show up with a bottle of wine). To make the evening even more romantic, ask your date to come over and *help* you cook. That way it becomes a team effort. And since you're now a team, you can even ask her to stop by the store and pick up a few things: "On your way over would you mind grabbing some fresh arugula . . . and Bud Light?"

If you can't cook, you can surely order restaurant delivery or carryout—which may be even better. Just make sure you serve the food on real plates and set the table with fresh flowers. Either way, you get to spend quality time with your date and you don't have to drive.

You and your friends meet up with her and her friends. This is an exciting car-free date because on the way there you can ride with your friends, and if things work out, you can ride home with her. There's no pressure because each party knows if they're not interested, they can just walk away. Plus, each person has friends there as a built-in support system.

Invite him over to watch his favorite TV show on your big screen. To make this work, you better actually have a big-screen television. This technique almost never fails when you sweeten the deal with pizza and beer. Sushi and sake might be a better choice, depending on the person.

Ask her to drive. This is the direct approach. Just invite the person out on a date and say, "Of course I'll pay for everything, but I don't own a car. Would it be possible for you to drive?" You'll probably feel a bit uncomfortable the first time you ask this. But that feeling will evaporate the moment she says, "That sounds fair." You will be successful in getting the date, but she'll probably ask you about it when you get together.

CAR-FREE DATE IDEAS

When you own a car it's easy to fall into a boring dating rut—dinner and a movie *again*? Car-free dating, however, encourages you to think creatively, to focus on each other, and to enjoy simple pleasures. Below is a list of date ideas that you should be able to do without a car.

- Take a walk at sunset—bring your camera and snap a few photos.
- Go for a bike ride—with the money you'll be saving you can buy his-and-hers bicycles.
- Have a backyard grill-out—no need to drive anywhere.
- Go in-line skating—show her your favorite five-mile route around your neighborhood.
- Exercise together—attending the same yoga class can be very sexy.
- Have rooftop cocktails—a creative way to have drinks if you live in an apartment building.
- Run or jog together—see what kind of shape he's really in.
- Cook dinner together—food can be so sensual.
- Play tennis in the park—always have two rackets and a can of tennis balls.

CAR-FREE IN CHICAGO, ILLINOIS

Being car-free has, if anything, improved my social life. On a simple level, I have met people on organized bike rides and just walking down the street. On a more complex level, staying in shape and being outdoors has made me a more confident person. I now feel more comfortable in social settings. And I haven't lost any friends because I don't have a car. Plus, car-free dating is great. You see more of the city together. And what's better than cuddling up with a romantic interest over hot chocolate after a long winter walk?

—Jennifer McArdle, 26, production manager

- Invite her for a swim—many condo and apartment complexes have pools.
- Have a DVD film festival—you each choose three movies, then hibernate all weekend.
- Organize a pub crawl—take a taxi so you're both free to party.
- Take a dance lesson—then invite her over to practice, practice, practice.
- Have a picnic in the park—many neighborhoods have a park or green space within walking distance.
- Do a 5K or 10K charity run—you can train together leading up to the race.
- Attend a sporting event—most are easy to reach by public transit.
- Read poetry to each other—you each bring a selection of your favorites.
- Share photo albums—a great way to learn about each other's childhood and family.
- Make wine or brew beer together—and then drink it together!
- Host a dinner party—invite some of your friends and some of hers.
- Attend church together—a good way to see if he has a spiritual side.
- Play a board game—see how competitive he is, and how intelligent.
- Have a backyard campout—set up a tent and sleeping bags outside.
- Have an indoor campout—set up a tent and sleeping bags in the living room.
- Go to a neighborhood church festival—easy to get to on foot or on bicycles.
- Attend a community parade—free entertainment often within cycling distance.
- Go to a museum—most are served by public transit.
- Visit a local library or bookstore—you'll learn a lot from what the other person reads.

This is merely a list of suggestions intended to spark your imagination. You'll soon find yourself coming up with your own creative, car-free dating ideas. And like all acquired skills, the more you do it the better you'll get.

WILL SOMEONE NOT DATE YOU BECAUSE YOU DON'T HAVE A CAR?

As you may have guessed, not everyone will be crazy about your car-free lifestyle. But based on my own experience, I would estimate that maybe 5 percent of people (one in twenty) won't go on a date with you simply because you don't have a car. Your results may vary. But as we all know, some people are into status and image. And some men and women do judge others by what kind of car they drive.

Here again, not having a car is advantageous. It will help you avoid dating people who are shallow, image-conscious status-seekers. After all, do you really want a relationship with someone who judges people based on what they own, instead of what kind of person they are?

Explaining Why You Don't Have a Car

Because we live in a car-centered culture in which everyone is expected to own a vehicle, eventually you will want to explain why you choose not to. Chances are the topic will come up in conversation sometime on the second or third date. So think about why it is that you choose to live car-free, and be prepared to explain. As food for thought, here is a list of common reasons people adopt a car-free lifestyle.

- "I live close to where I work so I don't need a car."
- "I ride my bike/my motorcycle/the bus/the train to work. So I don't need a car."
- "The lease expired on my previous car so I turned it back in. I'm now in the process of deciding whether I want another car or not."
- "My car kept getting broken into. I was so fed up I got rid of it."
- "I was using my car only once a week. I did the math and it just made no sense. So I got rid of it."
- "I have to park on the street and my car was constantly getting dinged and dented. I finally said the heck with it."
- "I believe in protecting the environment. And not owning a car is my way of reducing pollution."

- "I got rid of my car in order to live a healthier lifestyle. Now I ride my bike or walk to work. And I feel great."
- "I'm trying to save enough money to buy a house. So I got rid of the car expense."
- "I think cars are mostly a way to display status. And I'm not out to impress anyone."
- "Financial independence is more important to me than image."
- "I don't believe in blood for oil, which I think is the basis of U.S. foreign policy. So I choose not to be part of that equation."
- "I think the automobile industry and the big oil companies are ruining our country. So I refuse to own a car."

Any of the above reasons usually provides sufficient explanation to satisfy most inquirers. Over time you will become less concerned with explaining your decision to live car-free.

Develop Your Own System

Some of the strategies in this chapter may seem complicated or cumbersome to you right now. And in the first few weeks of going car-free you may hesitate to try them. But as you become more experienced at living without a car you will gradually develop a system that's comfortable for you. And you'll rapidly become proficient at arranging transportation that fits your social schedule and lifestyle.

CAR-FREE IN PORTLAND, OREGON

I live car-free and my social life is so busy I barely have an evening free. Let's take this week for example.

Tonight (Monday) I meet with colleagues at the Lucky Lab, a pub about three miles from where I work and about five miles from my house. If I am out past dark, I use a flashing front light on my bicycle and a red light on the back, and often a flashing light on my bag as well.

Tuesday I am meeting a friend for dinner in her neighborhood, about four miles from my house.

Wednesday at lunchtime I will meet a colleague for lunch downtown—it takes me ten minutes to get down there by bike, faster than by car probably, plus I don't pay for parking. After lunch there will be a meeting, also downtown, that I'll bike to, and will again park for free. The best part about parking a bike isn't the cash savings as much as it is not having to spend time looking for a spot! After work, I bike up to St. Johns (my old neighborhood) to work with an eight-year-old boy through a local mentoring program.

Thursday is free. Until recently I spent Thursday evenings teaching a writing workshop about ten minutes from my house at DePaul Treatment Centers' youth facility for high school boys in recovery from addiction. (I am finishing an MA thesis on Chinese lang. so I didn't renew my volunteer commitment so I could concentrate on the thesis; I'll probably work on that Thursday night—at least that is what I need to do!!)

Friday night I will meet friends to see a movie back in St. Johns.

Saturday a friend is in town and I will hang out with her, and also attend a training session (four to five miles from my house). My friend who is in town will stay in Beaverton, a suburb that I'll get to by biking to the Max (light rail), riding the Max out to Beaverton, and then biking to a place where we'll have brunch on Sunday.

I also have occasional dog-sitting gigs, potluck dinners to attend, music shows to go to, movies to see, etc. All without ever setting foot in a car!

I have never felt limited in dating without a car, either. My fiancé and I have dated car-free very regularly, though he has a car. The partner with a car can always meet in the person without a car's neighborhood. Or better, neither has a car, and you can meet wherever, and bike to where you want to go together, or walk, or bus, etc. Seriously, if someone doesn't want to date you because you don't have a car, what kind of a loser is that anyway? Not compatible with your lifestyle, and I bet on more than that one level.

—Amy Potthast, 32, manager of a non-profit

CHAPTER 23

Special Situations Require Creativity

"Creativity can solve almost any problem.
The creative act, the defeat of habit by
originality, overcomes everything."

—GEORGE LOIS, LEGENDARY ADMAN

If you're a lifelong car owner thinking about going car-free for the first time, you may be having skeptical thoughts, even a little anxiety. "If I don't have a car, how will I haul my kayak to the lake?" "How will I get my dog to the vet?" "What if I have a medical emergency?" The following are a few questions people commonly have about handling special situations, and some car-free solutions.

How will I get to the airport? All airports are served by public transit. If you can get to a transit stop you can get to your local airport. In fact, many people who own cars still take mass transit to the airport because parking there is so expensive. Many airports are also served by private door-to-door shuttles.

What about travel to other cities? Greyhound (www.greyhound .com) and Amtrak (www.amtrak.com) are both excellent forms of car-free interstate transportation. And both offer frequent discounts and special deals. I recently took Greyhound from St. Louis to Cincinnati for a long weekend for just $45. Renting a car with unlimited miles and paying for gas would have cost me twice as much.

How will I get my kayak to the lake, or move something really heavy? A kayak is light enough that you could easily transport several of them by bicycle, if you have the proper equipment. Take a look at the website www.bikesatwork.com. It offers tips on hauling heavy loads, and it has bike trailers for sale that are large enough to tow a small sailboat. According to www.bikesatwork.com, "Most people underestimate how much they can transport using their own muscle power. With the right equipment it is easy to move loads too large for an automobile."

If the lake is too far to reach by bicycle, or if you don't want to buy a bike trailer, you can always rent a vehicle. That's one of the benefits of renting instead of owning: you can get exactly the type of vehicle you need. In this case, a pickup truck, van, or SUV.

My friends who are really into kayaking go about eight times a year, so it's much cheaper to rent a vehicle than to own one for that specific purpose. Even if you rented a truck twenty weekends a year at a cost of $150 per weekend, it would still be way cheaper than owning one. And when you rent, you get a brand-new truck every time.

How will I get my dog or cat to the vet? Most public transit systems allow pets as long as they are in a pet carrier. Most taxi companies also allow pets in carriers, provided you notify the dispatcher when you call. Many people transport pets in a bicycle trailer (for large dogs), or in a bicycle basket (for smaller dogs and cats). Apparently the animals enjoy this type of travel.

For more information on bicycle trailers and baskets, visit www.burley.com, www.bicycletrailers.com, www.cycletote.com, or www.bobtrailers.com. One company, www.cynthiastwigs.com, specializes in comfortable bicycle baskets for dogs weighing up to twenty pounds. Another company, www.wicycle.com, sells trailers specifically built for dogs—the Wagalong Small Dog Trailer for pets under thirty pounds, and the Wagalong Large Dog Trailer for pets up to eighty pounds.

What if my local transit system doesn't allow bicycles? Most transit systems do allow bikes on board. But if yours doesn't, get a folding bike. When you get to the transit stop, fold up the bike, slip it into its custom-designed nylon carrying bag, sling it over your shoulder, and get on the bus. For more information on folding bikes, visit www.breezerbikes.com, www.dahon.com, or www.bikefriday.com.

Don't I need a car to go on vacation? With a little research you can find wonderful car-free vacations. Bicycling tours through wine country (www.trektravel.com), dude ranches in Wyoming, Caribbean cruises, hiking in Alaska, and beachcombing in the Bahamas do not require cars. There are myriad car-free travel opportunities, which you will now be able to afford since you don't have to pay for a car. Just do a Google search for "car-free vacations." If you decide you need a car for your getaway, rent one.

What if I need urgent medical care? We all hope we'll never encounter this situation. But if you do, keep a couple of things in mind. If you're injured badly when you're at work, out with friends, at a conference, or pretty much anyplace other than when you're home alone, someone else will take you to the emergency room. Even if you have a car at your disposal, when you're severely injured or suffering chest pain you should not drive yourself to the hospital. That could result in disaster.

For the same reason, if you're at home and you have a serious medical emergency, dial 911. An ambulance with trained paramedics can reach you a lot quicker than you can drive to the hospital. Even if you have a less serious medical emergency—like a cut, a broken bone, or a fall—again, you shouldn't drive yourself. Call a taxi or ask a friend to take you. This way if you get dizzy or pass out on the way to the hospital you won't be behind the wheel at the time.

Keep in mind, too, that if you drove yourself to the hospital, you'd have to park your car somewhere and then walk to the ER. So it's probably just as quick to wait for a taxi—which can drop you off right at the emergency room doors.

My wife is pregnant and we'll eventually have to rush to the hospital for the delivery. How will we get there? Luckily you'll have about nine months to plan a strategy for this one. The easiest solution is to lock in a low rate on a weekly or monthly rental car. Enterprise offers substantial savings with their "Month or More Rental Plan." This way you have a car sitting outside 24/7 during the several-week period in which the baby is likely to come, but you still don't need to own a car.

What if I can get there, but it's a real hassle? You may eventually realize that some of the things on your social calendar or your to-do list present bigger transportation challenges than others. Part of living car-free involves reevaluating, rearranging, and streamlining some of your activities for better efficiency. For example, you might find it difficult to get to your pottery class at the YMCA across town. If you've exhausted the transportation ideas suggested in this book, then you may want to consider some creative alternatives.

Part of living car-free involves reevaluating, rearranging, and streamlining some of your activities for better efficiency.

You could look for a new pottery class closer to home or near a transit stop. You could consider buying a pottery wheel of your own and turning your garage into a home studio (since you no longer need it for a car). Or you might consider taking up a new hobby altogether. Perhaps there's a glassblowing studio or an artists' guild in your neighborhood.

The Option of Last Resort

Taxicabs are a convenient form of twenty-four-hour transportation. Unfortunately, they're also expensive (though still far cheaper than owning a car). I don't recommend using taxis often, but in certain situations calling a cab makes sense.

It's a good idea to keep the phone numbers of two taxicab companies handy; if the wait is too long at one, call the other. In my years of being car-free I have used taxis only a handful of times—never because I was desperate, always because I was going out partying and I didn't want any of my friends behind the wheel.

And finally, if you have car sharing in your area, of course that will solve virtually all car-free problems.

PART FOUR

Living Well
without a Car

CHAPTER 24

Try Going Car-Free for One Week

"Always bear in mind that your own resolution to succeed is more important than any one thing."

—ABRAHAM LINCOLN

By now you've researched alternative forms of transportation, found ways to make your errands come to you, and thought about using creativity to overcome car-free obstacles. It's time to put everything you've learned into practice. I want you to place your car keys in a drawer for one full week (including the weekend). Try not to use the car at all. What you're after is a sense of whether or not car-free living suits you. Could you visualize your life without a car?

The Trial Week

It takes a little experience to figure out car-free living, so don't expect things to go perfectly smoothly right away. Here are a few tips that might help during the trial week:

- Leave fifteen minutes early for work on Monday morning to allow plenty of time for unexpected delays.
- Borrow needed equipment—like a bicycle or rain suit—instead of buying it.
- Make sure you have cell phone numbers of friends, relatives, and coworkers.
- Verify that your triple redundancy system is in place.
- Go for it and have fun.

Evaluating Your Trial Week

So how do you determine if the trial week is a success? More important, how can you tell if car-free living is a good fit for you? Here is a list of questions to think about during this trial period:

- Did you get to work on time?
- Were you more stressed or less stressed?
- Did you feel a sense of accomplishment?
- Did you ever feel isolated, stranded, or cut off?
- Did you see your friends and family more or less?
- Did you miss your car a little, a lot, or not at all?
- Do you think you could live well without owning a car?

CAUTION: Don't Expect the Payoff Just Yet

The big payoff of living a car-free lifestyle comes *after* you get rid of your car. That's when your expenses will shrink and your bank balance will surge. Of course, living car-lite has many financial benefits, too. But as long as you have a car parked outside you still have to deal with it, worry about it, maintain it, insure it, and pay for it. So during this trial week the tremendous peace of mind and financial freedom that come with car-free living will *not* materialize. Keep that in mind as you evaluate the trial.

Decision Time

If you made it just fine without your car during the trial week, it's time to go on to the next step. You now have to decide if you want to *gradually* adopt a car-free lifestyle, or take the plunge and get rid of your car right away. Both options have advantages and disadvantages.

Some people feel more comfortable easing into a car-free lifestyle by gradually reducing their car use over time. This makes sense for anyone who is still uncertain about whether they'll like car-free living. It provides a convenient safety net while they experiment with car-free transportation. This plan also makes sense for anyone who might have a difficult time buying a new car after they've sold their previous one, in case they later decide car-free living is not for them.

The disadvantage of easing into a car-free lifestyle is that you won't reap the big financial rewards of not owning a car. Because as long as you own one you still have to care for it and pay for it. Plus, if you always have a car parked outside, it may hinder your efforts to embrace car-free alternatives.

The advantage of taking the plunge and selling your car right away is that you will begin to see the financial and lifestyle benefits almost immediately. No more car payment. No more car insurance. No more paying high gas prices. You might even make money on the sale of your car.

On the downside, when you get rid of your car you will probably have to buy a transit pass or a bicycle, or both; so there will be some initial expense in making the transition. Plus, once your car is gone it will take some time and effort to replace it if you decide car-free living is not for you.

But remember that even if you sell your car you are not locked in to anything long-term. Ending your car-free experiment is as simple as buying another car. So if you're undecided, I suggest you go for it. Give it a couple of months. If you later determine car-free living is not for you, you have an easy exit strategy. You could even rent a car for a few weeks while you shop for a new one.

What If the Trial Failed?

If the trial week does not go well, don't give up. Instead, identify the trouble spots. Then go back to the previous chapters of this book that pertain to those topics. For example, if your commute by public transit took too much time, go back and review both chapter 9 ("Should You Move Closer to Where You Work?") and chapter 10 ("Mass Transit").

Once you figure out why the trial failed, you may determine that some lifestyle reengineering is necessary. Brainstorm about what changes you could make to facilitate a car-free lifestyle. Whatever obstacle lies between you and living car-free can be overcome. It may seem like a major effort is required in the near term, but the long-term payoff will be worth it.

CHAPTER 25

Taking the Plunge:
Getting Rid of Your Car

"It is our choices that show what we really are, far more than our abilities."

—J. K. ROWLING, AUTHOR

Selling your car will be the last hassle of car ownership you'll ever have to deal with. If you lease your car, don't worry; there is a way out of that, too.

Six Simple Steps to Selling a Car

By following the six steps in this chapter you can get rid of your vehicle and be on the car-free path to financial freedom.

STEP ONE: DETERMINE YOUR CAR'S VALUE

First, visit the Kelley Blue Book website at www.kbb.com. If you know your car's mileage, exact model, engine type, and options, Kelley Blue Book will tell you what it's worth. Another good website for establishing your car's value is www.edmunds.com. You should also check local newspaper classified ads to see what other sellers are asking for similar cars in your area—convertibles are cheaper in Minnesota than in Florida.

STEP TWO: RUN AN AD

I suggest running a classified ad in your local newspaper *and* listing your car online. According to J. D. Power and Associates, 54 percent of used-car buyers shop online.

Websites for selling your car include www.autotrader.com, www.cars.com, www.autobytel.com, www.carsdirect.com, www.craigslist

.org, and www.motors.ebay.com. The benefit of online listings is that you can include digital pictures of your car. This is a *huge* advantage.

STEP THREE: SET THE APPOINTMENT

The primary purpose of running an ad is to get potential buyers to call about the car. Be prepared to answer their questions. But your sole objective in this phone conversation is to set an appointment to have them come see the car in person. The odds of someone buying the car without seeing it first are slim. So ask them to come take a look.

STEP FOUR: PREPARE FOR THE TEST DRIVE

Once you have an appointment scheduled, make sure the car is immaculate. Clean it inside and out, and make any necessary repairs. When prospective buyers come to look at the car, ask them to drive it. According to Eric Satchwill, a career car sales professional and Mercedes-Benz dealer, "Your odds of selling any car go up dramatically if they test drive the vehicle. Without a test drive, you probably won't make the sale."

STEP FIVE: ASK THEM TO BUY IT

This is referred to as "closing the sale." It's as simple as saying, "Would you like to make an offer?" At this point, be prepared to negotiate on price. Few cars sell for the price listed in the original ad. Establish ahead of time what your bottom-line price is and stick to it. On the other hand, it's usually not worth turning down a serious buyer over a difference of a few hundred dollars.

STEP SIX: COMPLETE THE SALE

Once you have a legitimate offer, ask for a deposit. Then discuss the terms of completing the sale and form of payment. Follow the rules in your state for transferring the title and preparing the proper paperwork. The website www.autotrader.com has a link to every state's motor vehicle department website, a useful resource for this step.

Additional Resources

Both www.edmunds.com and www.kbb.com are excellent resources for selling a used car. They each have in-depth articles titled "Ten Steps to Selling Your Car." I suggest reading both of these articles. You'll find them under the "Advice" tab.

Getting Out of a Lease

According to www.leaseguide.com, one-third of all car leases are terminated early. There are two ways to do this. You can contact the leasing company and ask for the current lease payoff amount. Then you just mail them a check, and they'll mail you the clean title to the vehicle. Any lease can be terminated in this way. But beware that there may be additional fees to end the lease early, and you may have to pay sales tax. You will find more information on your lease contract under the heading "Early Termination."

In many states, this process also works with a third-party buyer. When you sell your leased car to a third-party, the buyer makes his check payable directly to the leasing company. The leasing company then transfers and mails the clean title to the new owner. Your leasing company will provide detailed instructions for execut-

CAR-FREE IN VICTORIA, BRITISH COLUMBIA

My wife and I have been weaning ourselves from a car over the last few years. We both owned cars as recently as four years ago, then I sold mine and we shared my wife's car. We sold her car two years ago, and shared some of the expenses on our son's car until this April, when we went cold turkey. My wife and I estimate we are conservatively saving $3,000 to $4,500 a year by not owning a car, which we are using to pay off our mortgage early. We anticipate retiring in the next three years. So far it has been an interesting experience. We will reevaluate our decision as we approach retirement. In the meantime, as long as we find we use alternatives very little (taxis, buses, and rental cars), we have had no burning need to buy another car. And the extra money is allowing us to set more important priorities in our life.

—Brian Collier, 53, government administrator

ing this process. Be sure to follow the instructions to the letter. Any overlooked detail could cause delays. Be very clear that you want the new title issued in the *buyer's* name, not yours. Check your state's DMV laws to make sure a third-party lease purchase is allowed.

Another option for getting out of a lease is using a website like www.swapalease.com or www.leasetrader.com. These websites match people who wish to exit their car lease early with buyers who wish to assume a short-term lease on a vehicle. Both of these websites offer detailed instructions to walk users through the lease transfer process. Transferring a car lease usually does not require paying early termination fees to the leasing company. But Swapalease.com and Leasetrader.com both charge fees to use their services.

What If I Owe More Than My Car Is Worth?

When I decided to sell my Toyota Sequoia, I had ten months left on a three-year lease. The bank said the payoff amount was $24,829. But the buyer was only willing to pay $23,800. That meant I would have to pony up $1,029 of my own money to get out of the lease. Ouch!

It seemed like a lot of money at first. But then I did a few calculations. In two weeks I'd have to make another car payment, $470, and another insurance payment, $133. In three weeks I'd have to pay my monthly parking, $120. And the 30,000-mile service on the car was coming up soon: $600. When I added it all up, it made sense to me to write a check for $1,029 to the bank, instead of shelling out $1,323 over the next several weeks.

You'll have to do the math for your own situation. But chances are paying a little to get rid of your car is a good investment. A one-time expense now will allow you to reap huge rewards month after month into the future.

CHAPTER 26

The Payoff: A Richer, Healthier, Less Stressed Life

> *"Everyone in my office thinks I'm in my late twenties when I just turned forty! It makes me feel great. And when you feel good, other aspects of your life are affected also."*
>
> —COLIN TURNER, CAR-FREE BICYCLE COMMUTER

My brother used to be a serious designer-coffee addict. He would stop at Starbucks at least twice a day. Despite years of lecturing him about the negative health effects of his habit, I was never able to convince him to give it up. Then I tried a different tactic; I showed him how much money he was blowing on his latte fetish (about $200 per month). That convinced him to give it up cold turkey.

Months later he told me about the many unexpected benefits of no longer being addicted to coffee. In addition to saving money, his teeth were whiter, he was sleeping better, he lowered his blood pressure, he was less moody and irritable, he no longer got the mid-morning jitters, he didn't have coffee breath, there were no more coffee stains on his clothes, so his dry cleaning bill was lower, and he felt better about not filling up the landfill with paper coffee cups.

Giving up car addiction is similar in many ways. Financial savings might be the initial motivating factor, but there are dozens of other benefits that come along with kicking the habit.

CAR-FREE IN PORTLAND, OREGON

I'd say the financial payoff is that it allows me to live quite comfortably on less than $20,000 a year.

—Daniel Lerch, 30, graduate student

The Benefits Add Up

You may experience some, many, or most of the following benefits by going car-free: Many of them you would never predict, but you'll sure notice them when they materialize.

FINANCIAL BENEFITS

- Slash your monthly expenses
- Have fewer bills to pay
- Pay off your credit cards
- Become debt-free
- Save for a down payment on a home
- Build an investment portfolio
- Face fewer unexpected expenses
- Pay off your mortgage early
- Maybe even become a millionaire

LIFESTYLE BENEFITS

- Spend less time sitting in traffic
- Deal with less aggravation
- Get to know your neighbors
- Work less because you spend less
- Have a built-in excuse for things you don't want to do

PHYSICAL BENEFITS

- Get more exercise
- Improve your health
- Sleep better
- Burn more calories
- Develop a firmer butt and thighs

CAR-FREE IN HARTFORD, CONNECTICUT

Not owning a car has allowed me to create a simplicity to life that I was not able to do while using a car for transportation.

—Dr. Malaika Sharp, computer science instructor and martial arts instructor

"EVER NOTICE THAT THERE ARE NEVER ANY MENTIONS OF BICYCLE RAGE OR PEDESTRIAN PILE-UPS?"

EMOTIONAL BENEFITS

- Have fewer responsibilities
- Have less to worry about
- Have less to remember
- Lower your stress level
- Find it easier to relax
- Know you're helping the planet, not hurting it

The Most Valuable Benefit

Perhaps the most valuable benefit of car-free living is peace of mind. It comes from the cumulative effect of the many smaller benefits listed above. For example, solid personal finances and good health are essential to peace of mind. And peace of mind is the foundation for building a high quality of life. When you get rid of your car you may find that all these benefits add up to one big payoff: a richer, healthier, less stressed life.

CAR-FREE IN SANTA BARBARA, CALIFORNIA

Living car-free means less to worry about. I don't have an expensive "investment" sitting out in the parking lot that someone could break into, crash into, or steal. Life is a bit simpler. I feel I have gotten rid of an "addiction" that took up time and wasted money.

—Garrick Sitongia, 43, electrical engineer

CHAPTER 27

Giving Back: What to Do with That Extra Time and Money

"In charity there is no excess."

—Sir Francis Bacon

It is the opinion of this author and many others that true personal fulfillment can best be reached when life includes a component of community service and charitable giving. This chapter offers a few suggestions for giving back some of the money and time you'll be saving by not owning an automobile.

Donate 10 Percent

I'm not suggesting you donate 10 percent of your annual salary to charity. Rather, I am suggesting you donate 10 percent of the money you're saving by not owning a car. The calculation is easy. Start with the total annual cost of your car, which you computed in chapter 2. Then subtract the estimated annual cost of your alternative modes of car-free transportation.

For example, let's say your car cost $6,000 per year, but to live car-free you bought a bicycle for $500 and an annual transit pass for $500. The amount of money you're saving by living car-free in that first year would be around $5,000. So find a few charities that are meaningful to you and divide $500 in donations among them.

Researching Charities

If you don't already have charities that you regularly support, here's a good way to find some. Charitable giving should be meaningful and personal. So think about what's important to you, and look for charities related to those areas. If you're a surfer you might support

charities that fight for cleaner oceans, like The Ocean Conservancy or Heal the Bay. If you're an animal lover you might support Greyhound Rescue or your local no-kill animal shelter. If you like to hike and camp, look into the Sierra Club.

One of the best resources for charitable giving is the website Charity Navigator (www.charitynavigator.org). This organization keeps a database of 5,000 charities and rates them on fiscal responsibility and effectiveness. Plus, you can browse for charities by region or by category. Charity Navigator is a good first stop if you're looking for a new nonprofit organization to support.

Volunteer Your Time

Once you get into the rhythm of car-free living, you will probably have extra time in your week. So why not volunteer at a local charity? Volunteering is a form of charitable giving. But instead of giving money, you give part of yourself. It's a guaranteed way to feel good and know you're making a difference in the world. After all, time is a far more valuable resource than money.

You can always volunteer to cook, clean, or wash dishes at a soup kitchen. But a better plan is to find a way to leverage your talents for the good of the charity. If you're a salesperson, volunteer to help with fundraising. If you're a doctor, hold a free clinic once a month at a local homeless shelter. If you're a journalist, write a few articles for the organization's newsletter. In other words, try to find a volunteer opportunity in which you can use your skills to have the greatest impact.

To find volunteer opportunities in your community, contact your local United Way office or call their volunteer center at 1-800-VOLUNTEER. Most United Way offices have a website that lists organizations in need of volunteers. You can also find places to volunteer through your employer, church, local nursing homes, or hospitals.

Living Car-Free Makes Giving Possible

Volunteering and giving money to charities is one of the most fulfilling aspects of my life. I couldn't do nearly as much of it if I had a car to pay for and look after. Giving can be a tremendous source of personal fulfillment for you, too.

CHAPTER 28

Advice for Two-Car and Three-Car Families

"If you would be wealthy, think
of saving as well as getting."

—Benjamin Franklin

I know, I know. Soccer practice, dance recitals, parent-teacher conferences, piano lessons, the dog needs shots, and so on. A parent's work is never done, and you could never get it all done without at least two cars in the family, right? I've heard this dozens of times from busy moms and dads. And for millions of families it may well be true.

But for millions of others it's not true. Often one of the two family cars is used almost exclusively for commuting and stays parked all but sixty minutes a day. Is that really an efficient use of the family's resources?

CAR-LITE IN SALT LAKE CITY, UTAH

We used to be a two-car family. Now we're a one-car family. Running around town and doing errands are actually quite easy. I think the secret to successfully being car-lite is attitude. I do not see this as being a hassle. I think of the bike first as transportation and the car a distant second.

Because of the money saved from having only one car I am able to work a three-quarter workweek, which I have done for the past six years. One less car also helped us pay off our mortgage in eleven years instead of fifteen. I then took the former house payment and put it into CDs, home improvements (not needing financing), and some Roth IRAs. Housing is crazy here in Salt Lake County. I estimate that what I put into home improvements in the past two years has increased in value by 50 percent. As you can see, there is a definite compounding effect initiated by not buying a second car.

—Louis and Julie Melini, physician's assistant and forensic nurse

Sadly, having two cars is something many married couples do simply because it's the American way. We are so accustomed to multiperson, multicar families in this country it's hard to imagine anything less than two cars in every driveway. The result: most couples needlessly spend thousands of dollars each year on a second car, when all they really need is a little lifestyle reengineering.

It Can Be Done

The city of Seattle, Washington, conducted a study called The One Less Car Challenge. They asked families to volunteer to park one of their cars—or their only car—and not use it for two months. According to the city's website, "Over eighty Seattle households parked their second or only car for eight weeks and provided detailed info on every trip they took. 100 percent of the households succeeded in not driving the extra car! After the study 15 percent of the households decided to sell their extra car because they determined that it was not worth the cost—they could get around just fine by owning fewer cars and using the bus, their bike, walking, etc."

Living with One Less Car

There are three keys to living with one less car. First, one of the two working adults in the household should find a way to commute car-free. This leaves the family car available for others to use.

CAR-LITE IN ITHACA, NEW YORK

In my family (two adults, two kids) we own one car. However, we resist the temptation to own two cars, which seems to be the norm with two working parents. The last two times we moved we made deliberate decisions to live close to work—even though housing was more expensive—specifically to reduce our need for a second car, and to enjoy the benefits of reduced car use. Right now we live in Ithaca, New York, which is a great place to go without a car. We also spent eight years in Palm Beach County, Florida (car country) and managed with only one vehicle.

—Fernando de Aragon, 46, staff director

Go back and read chapter 8 for a refresher on car-free commuting. If you have teenagers in the household, help them get summer jobs within walking or bicycling distance from home. Encourage them *not* to go into debt to buy a car of their own.

The second key is planning. If two people intend to use the car for different purposes on Tuesday night, there will be a conflict. A simple solution is to keep a large calendar on the refrigerator to mark down when the car is needed and by whom.

The third key is teamwork. Working together, being flexible, and communicating with your teammates will make sharing a car much easier. And like any team, after playing together for a while you'll be able to anticipate which teammate will do what and when. Eventually, your one-car household will become a smooth-running machine.

CAR-LITE IN CARLSBAD, CALIFORNIA

Families should realize how totally feasible living with just one car is—as long as you're willing to think outside the box. A lot of people get fixated on commuting in a certain way, and they don't even look at the alternatives. The best way to handle this is to choose to live close enough to where one person works that a bike or public transit commute is feasible.

Even if it's not in the cards to move right now, the next time the household packs up and moves to a new place for a new job, the location should be a priority. Even a relatively long commute can be done by bike, and it doesn't have to be every day. It's still doable to share a car with two driving commutes. One person can drop the other one off at work and pick him/her up. This requires some planning ahead, but once you get used to it, it's no big deal. My husband and I even did this pre-cell phone! You can even alternate who drops off whom.

Obviously the big "duh" for one-car commuting is if both people work at the same or adjacent locations. Drive in together, go home together. Again, it requires a little bit of coordination if one person has to go in early or stay later, but it's really not a big deal. And it's nicer to have company in the car anyway. Pretty much you just have to be willing to be a little flexible.

—Holly Ordway, 30, college English teacher

CAR-FREE IN PORTLAND, OREGON

Most people living in unhappy bondage to their car live in places that really do make it hard to give up the car. That's often the end of the discussion. But they moved there; they took jobs too far away. Of course, it's not trivial to change those things, but that doesn't make them any less worth changing. We are now enjoying the copious dividends of having been a double-income, car-free family for a decade.

—Todd Fahrner, 40, investigator

Do It for Your Children

Let's say you're a married couple and you have two one-year-old children. You're concerned because you know you're going to need a boatload of money to pay for college some day. Let's also say that giving up one of your two cars would save you $7,000 per year. If you invested $6,000 of that money in a trust fund and earned 8 percent per year, in seventeen years you'd have $240,000. That's probably enough to pay cash for college for both children. Who knows how much college will cost in the future, so why not sell one car and start saving now?

Imagine the peace of mind you'll have when you know your loved ones will be taken care of financially. I can't think of a better reason to stop spending money on a second car.

"I'VE BECOME DISILLUSIONED LATELY, MY NEW CAR HASN'T MADE ME SEXIER, WEALTHIER, OR SMARTER"

SPREAD THE WORD

Millions of Americans see automobile advertising every day and are convinced by its false promises and misleading claims. If the arguments in this book make sense to you, please help spread the word that every American does *not* need to own a car and that you *can* live well without one.

Share this book with anyone who you think might benefit from car-free or car-lite living. If someone in your family is looking for a way to simplify her life, tell her about this book. If you have friends or coworkers who constantly complain about money problems, suggest that they borrow this book from their local library. If you know someone who is struggling with debt or considering bankruptcy, *urge* him or her to read this book. And if there's a young person in your life who is about to go into debt to buy their first car, get them a copy of this book and *make* them read it.

Remember, buying or leasing a car, truck, or SUV is the single worst financial move most people make in their lifetime. Cars are destroyers of financial freedom, creators of debt, and decimators of savings. This book can't compete with the billions of dollars car companies have to spend on advertising, but with your help we can get the word out.

We Want to Hear from You

We want to know what you think of this book. Please email your thoughts, opinions, suggestions, comments, criticisms, and especially your car-free success stories to livecarfree@yahoo.com. Be sure to tell us if you got rid of a car or postponed the purchase of a car. And let us know if we have permission to publish your comments.

You can find additional information and resources about living car-free by visiting www.livecarfree.com or www.chrisbalish.com.

INDEX

ABOUT THE ARTISTS

Three talented artists contributed their work to this book. Their insight and creativity help illustrate many of the points made in the text, as well as poke fun at automobiles and their role in our society. If you'd like to learn more about the artists, please read their bios below.

Andy Singer's panel cartoon "No Exit" appears regularly in about fifteen papers, mostly alternative newsweeklies. His cartoons and illustrations have also appeared in such publications as the *New Yorker, Esquire, Progressive, Utne Reader, Boston Globe, Washington Post*, and many others. He is the author of *CARtoons*, a collection of cartoons and essays examining the economic, environmental, and social impact of automobiles, and *Attitude Presents: ANDY SINGER "No Exit."* For more of Andy's work, visit www.andysinger.com.

Sue Clancy markets her whimsical paintings, books, and cartoons through her business, This Artist Studios in Norman, Oklahoma. Her cartoons appear regularly in the *Oklahoma Gazette* and *Signews* in South Dakota, and her work has been featured in *Speedhorse* magazine and a number of other publications. You can see more of Sue's art at http://home.telepath.com/~artist/, www.jrbartgallery.com, and www.rit.edu/deafartists. Contact her at artist@telepath.com.

Dennis Draughon is a freelance cartoonist based in North Carolina. He was the last editorial cartoonist for the now-defunct *Raleigh Times*. From 1989 to 2004 Dennis was the staff editorial cartoonist for the Times-Tribune newspapers in Scranton, Pennsylvania. His work there earned a Fischetti Award for Distinguished Achievement in 1993 and the Association of America Editorial Cartoonists' 1999 "Golden Spike" award for the best cartoon killed by an editor. Dennis's work appears regularly in the *Durham News* and the *Fayetteville Observer* and is featured at www.editorialcartoonists.com.

ABOUT THE AUTHOR

CANDICE KELSEY

Chris Balish is an award-winning feature writer, reporter, and broadcast journalist. He began his writing career working for *Writer's Digest* magazine and Writer's Digest Books. Since 1995 he has been a full-time reporter and television news anchor. Chris is the recipient of nearly thirty awards for excellence in journalism and writing, including six regional Emmy Awards. He is a graduate of Dartmouth College in Hanover, New Hampshire.

But most important, Chris is passionate about how going car-free improved his life and how it can improve the lives of others. He commutes by bicycle year-round and travels all over on foot, on mass transit, and by carpooling with friends, girlfriends, and coworkers. Chris is single and has a vibrant car-free dating and social life. He does not own a car, and he's saving a ton of money. You can read Chris's full professional bio at www.chrisbalish.com.